NEAR DEATH EXPERIENCE

Millions have experienced it.

Many have kept the experience to themselves; others have waited years, or decades to speak of what happened.

Among the stories told, there are astonishing similarities.

A bright, almost blinding light, beautiful landscapes, vivid colors, a sense of peace and tranquility and the presence of a greater power.

But the one thing shared by all those who report NDE:

THEIR LIVES ARE FOREVER CHANGED

By the Light

LIONEL C. BASCOM
and BARBARA LOECHER

AVON BOOKS  NEW YORK

BY THE LIGHT is an original publication of Avon Books. This work has never before appeared in book form.

AVON BOOKS
A division of
The Hearst Corporation
1350 Avenue of the Americas
New York, New York 10019

Copyright © 1995 by Lionel Bascom and Barbara Loecher
Published by arrangement with the authors
Library of Congress Catalog Card Number: 95-94151
ISBN: 0-380-77801-7

First Avon Books Printing: September 1995

AVON TRADEMARK REG. U.S. PAT. OFF. AND IN OTHER COUNTRIES, MARCA REGISTRADA, HECHO EN U.S.A.

Printed in the U.S.A.

RA   10   9   8   7   6   5   4   3   2   1

᠅

To Luci,
who always said her children had options

We who are about to die demand a miracle.

—W. H. Auden

Miracles arise from a mind that is ready for them.

—*A Course in Miracles*

Contents

CHAPTER ONE

❧

Deliverance

I n working-class towns like Waterbury, summer nights in the 1960s meant going to firemen's carnivals down near the river, getting frozen custards or watching the Park and Rec games downtown.

Back then, everyone with a good paying job usually got paid by the hour to man the machinery of defense plants in booming Connecticut factory towns like this one in the Naugatuck Valley. It was the height of the Vietnam War. And there were still staunchly patriotic communities like Waterbury in an America that had grown weary of this undeclared conflict.

Softball and carnivals in the summer were as American here as doing doubles on the overnight shift was to meet expanding production at United Technology, Bardens and the other factories throughout the state. Any worker who punched a clock could earn a fat paycheck by doing piecework. Whether the plant produced starter switches for Titan rockets or assembly parts for Pratt and Whitney jet engines, the more you produced, the more you made. Some payrolls were still doled out in little brown envelopes with cash inside, because not everyone had a checking account in those days.

This was "Not Fonda Hanoi Jane" country, a widely known bumper sticker that condemned actress Jane Fonda's trip to Hanoi during the war. These were patriotic pockets where people felt betrayed by the antiwar movement.

They were ordinary people who would never celebrate war, but wouldn't condemn United States policy either. It was just unthinkable—the way driving a foreign car in Detroit was unthinkable.

People here made their living manufacturing ignitions, jet engines and the pieces that comprised the weaponry of a new generation of deadly nuclear submarines. And every one of these workers knew somebody who had joined the Marines, the Air Force or the Navy before his draft number was called. Joining up around here was still known as "going into the service," and everybody knew you weren't talking about the Peace Corps.

It was the same with calling in sick, a rare thing among the workers who rolled out every kind of weapon imaginable from high-caliber, armor-piercing bullets to helicopters. If you called in, you'd have to miss the game that night, because supervisors played and watched the games too.

On summer nights, the defense workers punched out and went home to pull on tank tops, sleeveless T-shirts and hip-hugging jeans like the rest of America. Then they went out to play. It would have been hard to find better-tuned V8s and simonized cars than those staggered throughout downtown parks at dusk. Guys in detailed pickups with mag wheels, running lights and maybe a rebel-flag vanity plate cruised the Park and Rec games.

Most guys played city-league softball after work under lights. Like the big leaguers, these boys of summer donned spikes and pin-striped uniforms too. They played for the glory of being in the industrial softball league, where a few hits got you a couple of beers after the game. The names of the various defense plants were scrawled across the front of jerseys; names like Grabowski, Brown or Stevens were slashed across the back.

All men were created equal at night under the lights. The only thing that mattered was how well you whacked the ball, not whether you got your hands dirty rolling brass or kept them clean making assembly-line engine ignition parts.

Like the guys in the neighborhood, Kathy Latrelle wore ski jackets with the names of pro ball teams on the back, and she rode a dirt bike on weekends.

But Kathy never seemed to quite fit into things around town, or anywhere else she went, for that matter—until after she died.

She'd always felt different, ever since she was a kid, growing up with a father prone to psychotic breakdowns, a brother who bailed out of the family early on and a mother who left her when she was only fifteen for an out-of-town lover. Later, there was Kathy's husband, who went off to Turkey without her. But that's another story.

In fact, you could say that dying was one of the best things that ever happened to Kathy. If you asked her, she'd say the near-death experience she had during a botched operation changed her whole view of life.

* * *

It changed Kate Valentine too.

Dying, she said, made her live for the first time. A bottom-line businesswoman, she nimbly climbed the ladder of a well-known nonprofit corporation and became its chief executive officer.

But after she died and went to heaven briefly, she turned to art. A woman who hadn't been able to draw a pumpkin before, she began painting landscapes in the style of the eighteenth-century decorative artists.

Kate didn't simply change careers, she gradually changed her life.

A grown-up Army brat, Mellen-Thomas Benedict wanted to become a famous feature-film maker. After high school in the South, he took a job in advertising. Within a year he was working the camera on car-crash movies and horror flicks.

He liked the work. The movies were a little light on substance. But so what? It wasn't as though he was on some quest for spiritual enlightenment. He was interested in entertainment.

That all changed after he too died and survived a near-death experience. He came back from death—after a trip through a sublime light—a changed man.

Once a cynic convinced that people were God's most serious mistake, he returned with an abiding love and compassion for others. He came back also with the ability to return to the light at will, to access information he could use to invent things and counsel others.

No longer interested in making movies, he began a spiritual journey that took him to the jungles of the Philippines, where holy men were said to work magic and heal the sick with faith.

*   *   *

Tattoos covered Steve Price like an inky blanket, eighty of them at last count. But this bulky, former Marine Corps sergeant would become teary-eyed when talking about his near-death experiences.

A sucking chest wound from mortar rounds hurled Steve dangerously close to death in Vietnam. Later, on a stretcher at a United States military hospital in the Philippines, he had a second out-of-body experience. A part of him floated upward toward the ceiling and emerged into a bright light.

"The light is the brightest thing you have ever seen," he would later say. "It is a mother cradling her young baby with love, only a million times more than that, and that is all the love there is."

Steve was a Marine Corps lifer. But that career was cut short by his experiences. Instead of soldiering, he began a sometimes bumpy spiritual journey that would eventually put him on a course similar to the others in this book.

Soldiers were trained to kill. And when Steve Price couldn't do this for a living anymore, he suddenly had to survive a full year in combat. What triggered his almost immediate spiritual transformation? What stirred the pacifistic nature in this man? What started an often painful, uncertain, twenty-year journey for him?

Tom Sawyer had once bragged that he had not read a book since the seventh grade. After an accident near Rochester, New York, that pinned him under a truck, this upstate truck driver said he suddenly craved books and college-level courses in quantum physics.

Tom, like the others, had survived a near-death experience.

Later, on a national television show, he said he discovered a natural curiosity for science during his death experience and asked complicated questions about science. The answers he sought came to him from a being he said was God.

Others have had less dramatic transformations, but their lives were nevertheless changed in profound ways following an NDE. All said they had seen life after life and immediately lost their fear of death. These are the stories of ordinary people resurrected in our time.

Ever since Adam blamed Eve for their eviction from Paradise, the hope of a life after death has been a dream of all men and women.

The afterlife has been depicted by artists throughout the ages. The hope of a personal resurrection is a theme in the mythology of all cultures. This hope has always found its way into our literature.

In modern times, word that death is not what it appears to be has reached us through unconventional sources.

Aviator Charles Lindbergh said he lost any fear of death during his now famous 1927 transatlantic fight aboard the *Spirit of St. Louis*. In an autobiographical account published years later, Lindbergh described a spiritual experience of transcendence that closely resembles what now might be called a near-death experience.

Eighteen hours into the first nonstop, solo flight from New York to Paris, Lindbergh said he suddenly experienced an altered state of consciousness. He felt that he was no longer merely flying. Instead, an awareness came over him that he was spreading through space, not flying in some small, narrow slice of it. Simultaneously, he felt as if he were spreading over the earth and into the heavens, able to transcend time and matter.

While all of this was unfolding, Lindbergh said he became the unwitting pilot for transparent, ghostly beings who helped him navigate. They solved problems of speed and direction and they gave him messages unaccessible in ordinary circumstances. This would later be reported repeatedly by thousands claiming to have had near-death experiences.

As the flight continued, Lindbergh said the weight of his own body disappeared and he felt close to these guardian angels, who had come to him from realms beyond earthly fields. This claim is similar to what has become known as the out-of-body experience.

It was during this out-of-body experience that he said a revelation came to him.

It was this:

"Death no longer seems the final end it used to be," he said, "but rather the entrance to a new and free existence."

Around 1945, psychologist Carl Jung suffered a near-fatal heart attack, and wrote of it later in his book, *Memories, Dreams, Reflections*. In it, Jung described what would now be called a classic NDE.

Writer Aldous Huxley made similar claims throughout his life. He too had experienced transcendental awareness and wrote about it in a piece called *The Doors of Perception*. Huxley said anyone who has a similar experience will never be the same. They will somehow be wise but humble; they will be happy but more curious. More than this, he said, they would emerge with ways to understand and to reason beyond ordinary means.

These words describe Steve Price, Kathy Latrelle, Kate Valentine and Mellen-Thomas Benedict, all near-death survivors. Their lives, like those of thousands of others, were changed in dramatic but not necessarily material ways following their experiences with death.

A 1982 Gallup poll indicated that more than eight million Americans acknowledged having NDEs. That number increases daily as more sophisticated medical procedures allow doctors and nurses to bring more of us back from the brink of death.

No one has isolated how many claim to have undergone subsequent lifestyle changes. But there is mounting evidence that one of the significant aftereffects of the NDE is a dramatic shift in values and a subsequent, clear-cut lifestyle change.

In many who survive NDEs, a concern for material things gives way to a longing for spiritual fulfillment. The transformations that follow can disrupt once-tranquil lives. Survivors often return to find that long-standing relationships no longer hold together; solid careers no longer seem worthwhile.

But those who make it through the transition—which can occur instantly or take decades—seem able to overcome previously insurmountable obstacles.

Even lost souls once bound for premature death from drug overdoses or from lethal drinking find spiritual anchors sometimes in churches, although many say God lies outside organized religions.

How? Where do this strength and previously absent abilities come from?

The NDE, we have been told, allows experiencers to view their lives with different perspectives. When your view of life or death is tilted in this way, they tell us, a different kind of understanding follows.

During and after an NDE, murderers say they felt the simultaneous pain of dying and killing all at once. And instead of suffering the overwhelming guilt you might expect, once-incorrigible criminals claim to understand both their victim's suffering and their own pain for the first time.

Rape victims who later survived NDEs say they relived both their own assault and the pain suffered by their rapist during the NDE.

Adults brutally beaten by their parents as children say they are able to view and relive both their own experience and their parent's torment simultaneously in the NDE.

This knowledge is transforming and perhaps liberating in ways only those who have experienced it can really explain.

For many, this brief encounter touches off a shift in values that can completely and thoroughly alter their lives.

What might this mean?

In her 1980 chronicle, Los Angeles writer Marilyn Ferguson identified hundreds of seemingly unrelated events that pointed to an unprecedented evolution in our time. The NDE phenomenon is just one of many Ferguson said would command widespread attention throughout the world in future decades.

Her book *The Aquarian Conspiracy: Personal and Social Transformation of Our Time* linked the claims of Aldous Huxley with the observations of psychologists Carl Jung and Abraham Maslow in ways that had never been done before.

To Ferguson it had become clear that a philosophical upheavel had gotten underway. Maslow was talking about a group of individuals he called scouts for mankind. These people, he said, would be irresistibly drawn to one another, whether they were businessmen, priests, poets or politicians.

In the 1970s, Marilyn said, "there were now networks of academics . . . lending their clout to the idea of evolving consciousness . . ." And this transforming vision was shared by many people. Clearly, Ferguson said, the world was experiencing a major philosophical shift and was finding one another.

Groups of people like those in this book claiming to have had NDEs began to find one another in just that way.

A loose-knit group of truck drivers, nurses, businessmen and gangsters joined housewives, public relations executives and psychologists who were telling similar stories about their experiences.

While these experiences shared any number of similarities, each one was different enough to remain unique and private, despite attempts to homogenize it.

As more and more people join a widening circle of individuals who survive an NDE, another single fact about the experience also seems to emerge among the survivors: they are transformed by the experience in calculable ways.

And this alone is a miracle in our time.

CHAPTER TWO

∞

Guns and Roses

He certainly looked dead. His skin wasn't just pale anymore; it was ashen, colorless. In the morning light, Tommy Golden had turned bluish gray, the real color of newborns before they get that first blush of life-giving air. The dead look like newborns too when life has gone out of them.

And that was how Tommy looked to his sister, Betty, that morning—dead.

This was a way out for Tommy, after years of trying; his way out would be what he liked to call Plan B.

And one cold morning in 1992, there was no pulse when Betty found him.

When she walked into his room, Tommy was already as cold to the touch as the pickup outside. Tommy's mouth was open, wide open, but he wasn't breathing. God only knew how long he had been this way. When she touched his wrist, even she had to admit her brother had really stopped his heart this time.

Tommy had really gone and done himself this time. That was how he would have described it.

"Taking myself out," he would have said, bobbing his head like the black soldiers he had known in 'Nam more than twenty years ago. "Gonna turn out the light this time," he had said just before the house got quiet the night before. But he had said this kind of thing so many times, how could Betty have known?

Yet this time the trip was different, if you believe Tommy's own account of what happened to him.

He said that although he appeared to be dead, there was something alive and stirring behind his dilated pupils. Deep down, in some place where consciousness lives, some part of Tommy Golden was still alive, he said after being revived. Even while Betty dialed 911, his spirit—the soul of Tommy, or whatever you want to call it—moved outside his dying body.

And as he lay dying, this entity lived, he said.

While the ambulance raced to the house through the country streets of Stafford, a working-class town in the eastern highlands of Connecticut, Tommy Golden, or some part of Tommy Golden, was literally "seeing the light"—if you believe the story he would later tell Betty.

As paramedics knelt to jump-start his silent heart or to push life-saving IV drugs into him, Tommy said he was being counseled by otherworldly beings, including his long-dead father. He was seeing a breathtaking landscape that others would later report having seen in similar experiences.

And if you believe the growing lore and clinical research into these things, not only did Tommy fail to die, he had a near-death experience and emerged into a loving, peaceful light.

Just over forty years old, Tommy had been trying for two decades to escape a hellish life that began unraveling for him in a Vietnamese village near Da Nang. Back home, Tommy couldn't even switch on a television set after the war without being reminded of Vietnam. A popular show called *China Beach* was especially eerie, since Tommy had been there and had his own story to tell about being in the region as a teenager.

For him, it automatically triggered real memories of Mai Lee, the dead child whose haunting brown eyes looked straight out from a fading, bent Polaroid Tommy carried around with him. He could still hear the rounds going off, still see his buddies in the 1st Marine Air Wing shooting into Mai Lee's village while his own rounds went off in the air above his head.

Tommy had started off his tour in Vietnam as a cocky Marine from a part of the States where it still meant something to join the service. Sailors and lance corporals who hitchhiked along Route 8 or up the Merritt Parkway always got rides in those days. So when Tommy came home with slogans like, "My rifle without me is useless. Without my rifle, I am useless," every man at the VFW or the American Legion downtown would salute what he was saying.

Tommy flew in-country for the first time in the fall of 1969. A bulk fuel man, Tommy had an assignment to refuel choppers at the Marble Mountain Air Facility not far from China Beach as part of the 1st Marine Air Wing. Sometimes he was thirty miles downriver at the An Hoa Combat Base, but in either case there was more than enough action, even for a gung-ho kid like Tommy, who had never run from a fight back in Enfield.

A long-nosed cartoon character named Kilroy became the symbol of World War II. Its droopy nose and bugged eyes could be seen etched on every available wall, truck fender and cave wall a soldier-artist could find. Below each drawing, the words "Kilroy was here" were usually written.

But the symbols of Vietnam were more personal and ominous for thousands of returning veterans. They came home with yet undetected cancers and genetic disorders that would disable them and their unborn children. These afflictions resulted from the widespread use of chemical defoliants made by American chemical companies. Untold thousands of combat veterans like Tommy returned with other ailments that went untreated or undetected. These included post-traumatic stress, related illnesses and drug addiction.

Heroin was routinely smuggled out of 'Nam in the body bags of dead American soldiers, then retrieved by mules who wrangled jobs in the morgues and mortuaries on Okinawa. Once retrieved, the drugs could easily be smuggled back into the United States aboard military flights so that passengers could enter the country without going through Customs inspections. Bricks of the stuff were shipped back home with street values running in the millions of dollars.

It was never clear when or how Tommy Golden became a junkie. One thing that did become clear was why he needed or seemed to need to use drugs. When Tommy got back, he kept telling people he had wanted to adopt five-year-old Mai Lee, the little girl whose picture he carried everywhere he went. Her parents had been killed and he used to bring her candy when he first met her in a village not far from base camp. In fact, he signed up for a second tour in Vietnam so that he could arrange her adoption, according to a newspaper account of Tommy's life in *The Hartford Courant.*

Those plans were tragically aborted one day in the fall of 1969.

Soldiers from Tommy's unit raided Mai Lee's village, not far from Da Nang. They captured a dozen VC and discovered a store of explosives under the porch of a house where American soldiers had often met with villagers. In a similar raid, Tommy's squad moved in to clean out suspected VC terrorists. While Tommy fired his weapon into the air, afraid he'd hurt the child, others in his unit weren't as careful. The Marines killed everyone in the village that morning.

Back home, Tommy still pulled out Mai Lee's picture every time he got drunk or high and told the story. He also liked to tell the story of one of his suicide attempts, the one that ended with his being evicted from heaven.

It happened that morning in the winter of 1992, when Betty found him damn near dead.

After answering Betty's 911 call, the ambulance swerved out into traffic along rural Route 190. Somewhere along the way to the ER at Johnson Memorial Hospital in Stafford Springs, the paramedics were able to snatch Tommy back to life. When his vital signs were stable again, they pumped his stomach, and doctors found all of his VA medications, plus some of Betty's heart medicines, this time.

"Betty, I am mad," he later told his sister, speaking from his bed in the psychiatric unit. "God didn't want me this time."

At this tiny hospital, Tommy might have appeared to be just another angry suicide patient who had botched it. But a closer examination of his life shows the traces of something profound.

During the experience, this tortured Vietnam veteran said that he was apparently blessed with a kind of otherworldly grace and got a brief glimpse of what some might call nirvana or heaven. He reported seeing a vivid white light that exuded total peace. But this gracious peace ended abruptly when he was visited by his deceased father, who told Tommy it wasn't his time. He, or his consciousness, was sent hurling back to life, and he awoke.

This is a classic NDE travelogue.

By the time Tommy had his NDE that winter morning in 1992, researchers like Ken Ring and Dr. Bruce Greyson had already written numerous books and papers about near-death experiences. In fact, Ring and his associates sometimes gave talks about the subject at Johnson and Memorial, so doctors and hospital staff there were familiar with NDE lore. Ring and Greyson had published many papers that outlined ways in which hospital personnel could recognize NDEs in their patients and help survivors cope. The researchers had also written about suicide and NDEs. So someone might have helped Tommy come to terms with his experience and understand that he hadn't been kicked out of heaven but that it just wasn't his time to go. Ken and Bruce worked at the University of Connecticut, in the same state where Tommy lived. Tommy didn't know that. Close as he was to help, he never realized it was there.

To believe you have been ejected from heaven must be the curse of a lifetime.

Steve Price once thought that he too had been kicked out of heaven. But Steve heard about Ken and Bruce and the mystifying experiences they called NDEs. After years of reading and talking about his experience, he understood that there were things he had yet to do in his life. The experience, and this realization, transformed him.

In Steve there were immediate changes in fundamental ways. It would just take him a longer time to understand it all. And fortunately, he did finally begin to understand it, with a lot of help from a widening circle of people in this new field.

But Tommy Golden wouldn't be so lucky. A clock that had been ticking since he returned from Vietnam would finally run out. Although he had returned to a state where the most intensive debates over the meaning of the NDE were being carried out at that very time, none of it reached him.

Raised in Enfield, about thirty miles northwest of Waterbury, Tommy had grown up with a kind of wholesale loyalty for God, country and bowling leagues.

When he returned to Enfield from Vietnam, Tommy came back the way many veterans did—hooked on heavy drugs and traumatized. Whether they came from the mean streets of the Bronx or from rural towns like Enfield and now Stafford, many were heroin junkies.

So if near-death experiences were transforming, Tommy was a prime candidate. But these shifts were often initially subtle, and the people who experienced them did not always embrace the encounters in positive ways. In fact, many, like Tommy, who saw what they described as heaven and were sent back, came back believing themselves unworthy and became severely depressed.

After one of his many tries to end his life, Tommy again found himself in a veterans' hospital in the summer of 1992, less than six months after his stay in Johnson and Memorial.

He kept scratching his wrists, irritated from the leather restraints doctors had ordered to keep him from hurting himself. The restraints taken off now, he sat up in his bed for the first time in what must have seemed like days since they brought him in.

It was just about one o'clock in the afternoon in the early part of July, and the doctors at the West Haven Veterans Affairs Medical Center were releasing him from Nine West again.

Tommy had a plan.

He'd been kicked out of heaven and he was sure he'd landed in hell. And hell, for Tommy, was right here on earth. An experience that had meant a reprieve for millions of others from early death had condemned Tommy to hell.

He had tried to kill himself on four different occasions and had wound up in the VA hospital the last time. After his examination by three people, including two doctors, Tommy's latest suicide ideation had seemed to pass, so they planned to release him the next morning.

Leaving his false teeth behind on a hospital nightstand, Tommy went downstairs until he reached the lobby, where Bobby Walker was hanging out. Tommy cashed a check for a hundred dollars at the hospital reception desk and told Bobby he was going to cop some smack and shoot it up in Oak Grove Cemetery across the street.

"I am going to do it all," Tommy said. "Going to do myself."

He also saw Bruce Brown, another friend, that afternoon, and he told Brown that he was going to kill himself.

"Go on back upstairs, Tommy," Brown reportedly told him.

"If they cared, I'd be up there," Tommy was quoted as saying.

He telephoned his sister, Betty. They spoke briefly; then he hung up abruptly. Then Tommy called a cab that took him to Congress Avenue and Arch Street in new Haven. It was one of the city's busiest drug supermarkets. He gave the driver a twenty and told him to wait. Minutes later, Tommy made the return trip. The driver dropped him off at a market across from the hospital and Tommy told him he was going into the graveyard.

After therapy, Bobby Walker headed down Spring Street, crossing Campbell Avenue looking for Tommy. He followed the green wrought-iron fence to the entrance of Oak Grove. Inside the gate, he began calling out Tommy's name, over and over again.

Walking toward an older section where some stones dated back to the Civil War, he came to a more remote spot. Bobby could hear the hum of cars from the interstate not far away. On a path that led to more dense woods, he finally saw Tommy through a clump of maple trees near the rear cement wall. He was lying facedown, his knees curled up toward his chin. His head and hands were pointing downward. He was lying there almost the way an unborn baby lies in its mother's womb.

Others in similar circumstances have said repeatedly that meeting Ken Ring, Bruce Greyson or other people who could talk to them about nearly dying often triggered difficult but worthwhile turning points in their lives. It happened to Kathy on her twenty-fifth birthday.

〜

CHAPTER THREE

Kathy Latrelle

Afraid to sleep, little Kathy was lying in bed, listening to her father down the hall. He'd been on the phone since three o'clock in the morning. That was when he finally stopped shouting, stopped pacing and dialed someone's number. Two hours had passed since then. Kathy could still hear him muttering and weeping into the receiver in the living room. She couldn't understand what he was saying. That didn't matter, though, as long as he stayed on the phone another hour or so, until morning, when she and her mother could get help.

It could have been much worse. But Kathy had seen this one coming and hidden the knives the day before. The pattern was pretty predictable now. It had been since her father started having his "nervous breakdowns." That was what the doctor called them.

Kathy was ten when it all started. It was 1967 now and she was thirteen. Her father only seemed to get worse. After a while, he could barely make it to work. It was a deepening cycle. First there were weeks of downward-spiraling depression that

he spent shivering in bed. Then there were days of
restlessness that led to the next furious rage.

The breakdowns usually came at night, and they
were terrifying. He'd turn on her and her mother,
accuse them of trying to murder him, ransack the
house looking for something—the knives, for all
they knew—until he exhausted himself. For a couple of days after, he'd sleep virtually without waking.

Kathy's twenty-year-old brother, Lloyd, never
seemed to be around for these episodes. He'd be at
his girlfriend's house or on a camping trip. This
time he was in the Marines in South Carolina, hundreds of miles from home here in Waterbury.

The wear of it all was beginning to show on
Kathy's mother. And it was taking a toll on Kathy.
Fair-skinned, with long blond hair, she'd show up
in school after nights of worry with dark circles
under her eyes. She and her mother had to keep
on their toes, predict when the next breakdown
was coming and get the knives out of the house to
the neighbors.

Even with the knives out of the house, Kathy
would lie awake nights like these, afraid to sleep,
afraid her father would find something sharp,
something they'd forgotten, and stab them to death
in their beds. That was her greatest fear. She'd lie
there afraid of dying, wondering why all this had
happened to them.

When she did die, of course, she knew. In death,
she briefly joined a white, bright light and began
to relive scenes from her life, not only as herself,
but as the other people who'd been part of them.
She was herself at thirteen again, lying in her bed,
the covers pulled up around her thin, exhausted

face, listening to her father on the phone down the hall. She was her mother, in her own bed, trying to figure out how they'd get through this breakdown, how she'd keep the family going, how they'd pay the rent. And she was her father, terrified, frantic, certain he'd been trapped, convinced they were plotting to murder him. When she died, Kathy knew how they all felt at those times. She felt it herself. And that made it easier for her to understand, and to move on.

The Waterbury neighborhood where Kathy grew up was a pragmatic, workaday place. It had none of the glamour of Connecticut's gold coast, where wealthy commuters lived in five-bedroom, faux Tudor houses with three-car garages for their Mercedeses and Lincolns. More or less in the center of the state, Waterbury filled out the larger part of the undulating Naugatuck River valley. The river had powered the first brass mills and continued to offer cheap means of disposing of the waste products of brass manufacturing.

By the 1950s, the city stretched for miles from the Naugatuck's oily banks, a grid of brick factory buildings and smokestacks; churches; Knights of Columbus and Portuguese-American clubs; woodframed, two-bedroom homes with on-the-street parking; a smattering of parks; few trees; and a green cluttered with war memorials.

Drawn by the prospect of steady work in the factories, immigrants from Italy, Poland, Albania, Greece and Hungary had settled in the city, built the homes, the churches, the neighborhoods and raised the children they expected to have good jobs in the factories one day too.

Kathy's family lived on a quiet road one block

from the nearest factory. Their four-plex looked like the neighbors', with the same modest lawn, the same Flexible Flyer sleds on the sidewalk in winter, the same bicycles in summer.

Kathy's parents had grown up in Waterbury. Both were from old Yankee families. Her father, Gilbert, had been born at home on the kitchen table.

In 1954, when Kathy was born, he was still working. He played and taught the accordion. During the day he'd teach. He had several dozen students in Waterbury. Evenings, he'd work at the clubs. Most of the nightclubs and restaurants in the area had dance bands. He played at places like the Hillside Restaurant, serenading the clientele—mostly factory workers in their going-out suits and dresses—with "Put Your Head on My Shoulder" and "Twilight Time." Weekend days, he'd squeeze in a few bar mitzvahs and weddings. He always wore a tux to work.

"Why do other kids' fathers have to rent tuxedos?" Kathy once asked her mother, admiring all the tuxes in her father's closet. He had five. Kathy always tried to catch a glimpse of him on his way to a job. He was slim, with blond hair and dark blue eyes, and to her, he looked good in a tuxedo. She resembled him more than she resembled her mother, who was also blond, but with very pale blue eyes.

Her mother always worked, which was fortunate, considering how things turned out. When Kathy and Lloyd were young, she worked for the Wheeler Wire Company soldering nose cones on the Titan II missiles. It was the Cold War, and President Kennedy had Titans aimed at Khrushchev's Soviet Union. Later she worked at a downtown uniform shop and then at another welding-and-soldering job. Finally, when Kathy was in high school, her mother went to nursing school and became a licensed practical nurse. She did the cooking and cleaning and laundry too, so she never had much time to spare.

Once, though, when Kathy was small, she took time out to decorate her daughter's bedroom. She painted the ceiling like the sky, and decorated it with glow-in-the-dark constellations. She painted the walls a lighter blue and added a green carpet to look like grass. Finally, she sewed curtains from a jungle print fabric, creating a room that was a small world of its own. Later, it would become a refuge for Kathy.

When Kathy turned four, she started kindergarten. Her teachers could tell she was bright. In fact, an IQ test they gave her in high school showed she was quite brilliant. She scored 145. The average score is somewhere between 90 and 110. But Kathy had a problem. She could never sit still. "The Beast," her parents called her when they came home from work tired and she couldn't settle down. They took her to a doctor, who concluded she was hyperactive. He prescribed Ritalin, which helped, but not as much as they had hoped.

"Sit still," her parents would tell her while she fidgeted at the dinner table. Both children had been raised on a literal interpretation of "spare the rod." When a warning didn't work, a spanking often followed. Kathy tried but never seemed to please her father the way Lloyd seemed to. She tried to emulate Lloyd. She idolized him. As a little girl, she often wondered whether her father would have found it easier to love her had she been a boy.

The hyperactivity made her feel as though she

didn't fit in. In school everything distracted her. She couldn't pay attention to her teachers. They seemed to go over the same lessons innumerable times. She'd lose interest, start daydreaming and snap to only when they'd reprimand her. So she started bringing books from home. She had hundreds of books. In school she would hide one behind her notebook and lose herself in the adventures of Nancy Drew.

While the teacher reviewed the math lesson she'd learned the first time around, Kathy could sit at her desk and read about Nancy Drew in *The Hidden Staircase* or *The Quest of the Missing Map*. She could lose herself in stories about Nancy's developing friendship with Trixie Chatham, a little girl whose father had died and whose mother rarely had time for her. Trixie lived in a house haunted by the ghost of a man with terrible eyes. Only Trixie could see him. But then Nancy arrived, saw him herself and discovered he was a real-life bandit prowling the house for a map that would lead to a buried treasure. Nancy finally found the map. Then she, Trixie and Trixie's mother sailed to the island where the treasure was buried and found a chest of gold coins and beautiful jewels.

When Kathy's teacher went over long division once again, she could look out the eight-foot windows of the elementary school, past the chain-link fence in the school yard, beyond the smokestack-spiked rim of the Naugatuck Valley. And she could imagine the island, bright and warm and welcoming.

The other kids in Kathy's class, the girls in particular, thought she was peculiar and let her know it. Not only was Kathy always in trouble, she preferred to dress like a tomboy, going to school in jeans, T-shirts and sneakers. The other girls, who sat quietly in their gingham dresses and Mary Janes, excluded her.

The one place she felt accepted and welcome then was the Methodist church. The minister never yelled or lectured. He made her feel she was perfectly all right. She tried not to miss a Sunday.

Adolescence would have been tough enough. By the time Kathy was thirteen, she was already five feet seven inches, taller than everyone in her class. She still wore her long blond hair parted in the middle. Very fashionable. But she was gawky and uncoordinated, always bad at sports, and self-conscious. By then, the kids in the neighborhood had found out about her father. They weren't sympathetic.

"Your father's in the nuthouse!" a boy on her bus taunted one morning while she stood in the aisle between the seats, trying to find a place to sit. The kids told the others at school, and before long, everyone knew her father was at a state mental hospital called Connecticut Valley.

So Kathy started spending more time alone in her room, reading and planning how to get away. She didn't want to go to college; she didn't like school. Her brother, Lloyd, had escaped by joining the Marines. She decided to join the Air Force.

It was an easy decision. Kathy's mother had signed her up for the Civilian Auxiliary Air Patrol, a volunteer group trained to help with search-and-rescue missions for lost airplanes. Her mother thought the experience would be good for her, and it was. Kathy enjoyed it.

So she made sure she passed all her classes at Kennedy High—which was easy enough, since she never had to study to do well. And she steered clear of trouble. No drinking. No drugs. No sleeping around. She didn't want to do anything to jeopardize her chance of getting into the Air Force and out of Waterbury.

And, she figured, she had enough problems without creating more. She wasn't going to make any excuses for herself either, the way her brother had. Lloyd had started using drugs, and Kathy was convinced he'd also started selling them. Her parents would never admit it, even when he had plants that looked suspiciously like marijuana growing in the pantry, but Kathy had to. She'd idolized her brother when she was a little girl. He always seemed to be so capable, so self-assured. When she heard he was dealing—everyone at school said so—she felt disappointed and betrayed.

If your life is really bad, you have to look at it and say, What is really bad? and you have to change it, she'd tell herself when the fear or loneliness was overwhelming. If you just hang out and let it happen to you, then it's your fault it's so bad, you stupid fool.

Kathy graduated from Kennedy in 1971. At the time, women had to be eighteen to join the Air Force and Kathy was only seventeen. So she got a job as a waitress at a coffee shop downtown and delivered newspapers for the *Waterbury Republican*. Two days after her eighteenth birthday, she quit both jobs and signed up.

"I can't wait to get out of here," she told her cousin Nancy, one of her closest friends since childhood. "I'm going to go into the Air Force and leave. I'm going to get myself an education and get my shit all together, and forget this."

*   *   *

Years after, though, she found herself thinking about that sleepless night when she was thirteen, listening to her father on the phone . . .

Eventually, she heard her mother walk down the hall and talk to him that night.

"Gil, why don't you come back to bed?" But he wouldn't. Her mother finally gave up and went back to bed herself.

At dawn, when the bit of sky showing through her bedroom curtains changed from purple to dark blue, Kathy climbed out of bed. She went to her parents' room and got her mother. They walked back down the hall together. They found her father near the couch in the living room, curled up in a fetal position on the carpet, sucking his thumb. He was incoherent. They called Connecticut Valley Hospital and the doctors sent someone.

Weeks later, her father came back home slightly depressed, exhausted and more gaunt.

And then the whole thing happened all over again. And it happened again and again. Sometimes it was ten months later. Or eight months later. Maybe fourteen months later. Each time they hid the knives. And Kathy stayed up nights thinking about how, if she lived, she would try to get away.

CHAPTER FOUR

〰

Kate Valentine

When her time came, Kate says she just lay down and was ready to die.

But something went awry.

A public relations executive and onetime chief executive officer for a major nonprofit organization, Kate was used to planning her life. Planning the end of her life was carried out in much the same way she had planned and executed any other campaign—with care and precision, paying close attention to the details.

Kate took care of almost every detail—except one. As the night closed in on her, she was still busy in her bed, writing notes to Paul, her husband, knowing these would be her last words. She had already arranged for her sister to take care of her three young children, little stairsteps at five, twelve and fourteen years old. The living will had been made out and all the insurance policies were in order.

Finally, she had written Paul last-minute notes on those little yellow stickum things, telling him how she'd like things after she was gone. Forget-me-nots, she called them.

So there was nothing left for this thirty-two-year-old woman to do that windy March night in 1980 but to lay her ailing, cancer-racked body down and expect to die. Her death that night would have culminated a six-year losing battle with thyroid cancer that had left her with an irregular heartbeat and severe circulation problems. She barely weighed ninety pounds and was emotionally exhausted.

I know I am dying, she thinks, telling herself it's all right to let go and die. A headache bored right through her thoughts, reminding her of all the things that had gone wrong with her body. Examining her aching hands and feet that night, she saw they were steadily turning blacker from being bloodless for so long. Even standing was painful, and walking had become nearly impossible now. So Kate was confined to the upper floors of their renovated Victorian home in an idyllic part of Connecticut, known as the Winsted section of Winchester, near the Massachusetts border.

Even the transplanted thyroid glands, which produced chemicals that controlled muscle tone, weren't working. So her body's largest muscle, the heart, was as out of whack as the rest of her that night.

No one has to tell me, she told herself quietly. I know I am dying.

Kate does not remember specifically what she did last. But she does remember this . . .

"A feeling just came over me that it's okay now. I did it all," she said, then closed her eyes.

"It was very black, not black like when you close your eyes, because this time there were no shadows. This blackness was all-pervasive," she said years afterward.

No, Kate did not die, even though her cancer and all the complications associated with it should have killed her, if you believed her doctors. Instead of dying, she was treated to the experience of her life.

"There was this burst of light. It was almost as if I were enveloped by it in an instant. It wasn't blinding, but it was so incredible," she said, her clear eyes sparkling with the memory of the experience. "It was brighter than anything I've ever encountered but did not make me squint. I went through something and came out into something," she said, unable to explain this part of the experience in any further detail.

"It was some sort of transition. It was sudden and there were two things going on: first, the colors were incredible, and there was this incredible sense of all-pervasive peace.

"There are no words to describe it," she said, repeating a claim made by many others who also claim to have had NDEs. "In some ways it felt like relief. But in other ways it felt as if I had finally come home, that I had gone back and everything that had once been important no longer seemed important to me in that light."

I found myself on this incredibly high precipice looking down on the most beautiful garden and valley I had ever seen. The first thing that struck me was the colors," said Kate. The colors were so vivid, she said, they made the countryside around Winsted look like the reverse side of a beautiful tapestry.

"No matter what I do, I cannot recapture the intensity of those colors now," she said more than a dozen years after surviving this experience.

"The second thing I was aware of was that someone was standing on my left-hand side, not a person you could see, though." She said she felt this presence the way you know someone is coming up behind you. "You can't see them or hear them, but you know they're there," she said. "This person was emanating this incredible sense of peace. It was like hearing the word 'peace,' but only it's being emanated to you, not spoken," she said. "I realized there was someone standing on my left side and I had a conversation, although not verbally." She said this telepathic talk was with God.

"I call the presence God, but I guess you can call it anything you want. I realized someone was next to me. I realized that I thought it was God," she said. All of this occurred simultaneously, or in some rapid-fire way that made time appear irrelevant.

"As soon as I realized that He was next to me, I was aware of the knowledge instantly," she said. "I was incredibly sorry for things I had done, instantly sorry, because the person sitting next to me radiated such peace and love. I realized how far I had to go and how little I had gone.

"But the essence of Kate, who Kate had been in this dimension, immediately went to her defense," she said. "I was instantly told no explanation was necessary. I was told it didn't matter."

Then she was awash in a wave of paternal love.

There, she said, you don't have to strain to understand anything, and you don't have to explain anything either.

"I felt everything I had ever done that had caused other people pain, things that were wrong," she said. Classically, this experience is sometimes called a "life review."

In hers, Kate said she understood what was wrong in her life. And since she claimed her personality remained intact during the experience, she repeatedly wanted to defend herself against the things she was reminded she had done. But each time, she said, she learned that even those things she believed had been wrong were now okay.

"Then I knew I wanted to stay," she said.

"In that dimension," she said, "we aren't separated from each other by our bodies. In the other dimension we are all one; it's cohesive, but each personality is intact. Whoever you are here is who you are over there. We go over with all of our warts, but all around you, it's accepted, and I think you are able to understand everything.

If there is any forgiveness in the next dimension, it comes from within, which is the way it should be in this dimension too, but we really haven't figured that out yet. In an instant, you know everything. I knew I could find out anything."

In the playback of her life, Kate relived horrific scenes from her childhood when she grew up in a Long Island, New York, family in which beatings and alcoholic binges were routine. Reliving those scenes, she said, allowed her to understand her parents and why they had treated her so badly. Even episodes in her young life that could later be described only as torture were understood after her near death, Kate said.

"A lot of it wouldn't mean anything to anyone but me, so I keep it to myself," she would later say. "I don't deal with that and I don't deal it out. At the moment, I knew all things and when I came back, I no longer knew all things," she said, taking what would become an uncharacteristic departure from a conversation that largely remained earthbound and practical.

"Where did Einstein find the theory of relativity?" she asks. "Where did Galileo find the information he found? Where did Mozart find his music? It's really not a place," she says, answering her own questions. "It's in here." She points to her own chest.

"All information, past, present and future, is available to you at all times," she says, with the conviction of a priest telling a worshiper to have faith in God. But this woman has no religious pretensions. She does not claim to be born again after her brush with death. In fact, she exhibits a kind of disdain for organized religious claims of godliness. God, she declares, is in us all. Claiming Him is a matter for individuals to sort out for themselves.

Kate says she knows the source of Galileo's and Mozart's genius. She knows, she says, because all genius large or small comes from some universal lake of thought and ideas. She too had apparently tapped into some reservoir of information during her experience in the light that now allows her to make art. Without ever studying art history or the quirks of distinct periods, she discovered techniques she initially believed to be her own but which later proved to be those of other, deceased American artists. They painted decorative art scenes from the eighteenth century. But they lived three hundred years before Kate was born.

So after her near death, Kate took up painting—once a hobby she had never perfected—and she developed a passion for eighteenth-century folk art. This was nothing less than a miracle for a business type like Kate, who previously had not been able even to paint or draw a recognizable pumpkin, according to her husband, Paul.

But during her experience, Kate says she saw rolling landscapes of lush green hills dotted with beautiful trees and flowers everywhere. She stood high above beautiful valleys.

"I wanted to go down into this valley," she says, "and I knew if I went into the valley, I could stay. I started this mental fight because I wanted to stay but knew I couldn't do it."

"I am going," she remembered saying, and also remembered being told instantly that she could not stay. "I remember doing this mental thing about staying, but it did me no good," said Kate. "I was aware I had the children at home to raise, and my husband, and I knew they would be okay. I was told I had to go back, but I was fighting to stay."

The next morning Kate awoke and noticed two things immediately. First, she was still alive. Second, she could breathe without audibly wheezing air.

"I could breathe in without pain. The pain had gone and, like a kid, I started testing it." As she took progressively deeper and deeper breaths, her once-infected lungs seemed to work without effort.

"How much do I have to breathe in before the pain comes back?" she wondered, but knew that somehow it would not come back. "I had this inner knowing that I was healed." Having been raised in a house where booze was the religion of choice, Kate says her belief system would not let her give credence to this kind of thing. "I didn't have the background and was spiritually unable to embrace this experience very well."

But the physical evidence was overpowering.

"My hands had turned pink overnight and looked normal for the first time in over a year," she said, interrupting an interview repeatedly to quiet Amadeus, her gangly German shepherd. "My body was working." She didn't know how or why, but her feet had also turned flesh-colored again and when she tried to use them, that pain was gone too.

"I just got up slowly by myself and sat on the edge of my bed and looked down at my toes," she said, knowing that she could again walk without that annoying, tingly, pins-and-needle twinge you experience when a foot or a hand goes to sleep. For more than a year, this tingle had constantly radiated through her legs and feet, but it was gone the morning after her godly experience.

"I started to walk about my room slowly and everything worked. Nothing hurt," she said.

But she noticed something equally new.

"I carried around this peace with me as if I had been sprinkled with some kind of fairy dust," said Kate, whose short, cropped hair is the color of salt and pepper.

Although she had not been able to venture downstairs in weeks, she climbed down the stairs unaided and walked into the kitchen, where Paul was busy cooking breakfast and getting the children ready for school.

"He turned white when he saw me," she said. "He has a scientist's mind and was thinking, Remission—Kate just had some kind of remission, and he went with that," she said. It was a remission, but not one that doctors would ever be able to explain.

"I just got progressively stronger," she said, also

not knowing or understanding what had happened to her.

"I didn't know. I knew I had touched something incredibly profound," she said, but kept the details to herself for years afterward. "It was so beautiful that I wasn't going to share it with anyone. I was also a realist and knew that if I said anything like, 'I had this crazy dream and it was connected with this cure,' people would start to put labels on me, and I was in a place in my life where I was not about to let anybody question my validity. I shared this with no one and there were no exceptions."

A physical done by her doctor a few days later confirmed what Kate and Paul already understood. Her cancer was in remission and all traces of it had disappeared.

"He told my husband I was in remission and that these things did happen. My thyroid was working. The transplants were working. He told my husband, 'These things happen. We can't explain them.' " They left Hartford Hospital believing that Kate had been reprieved. The couple picked up their lives where Kate's impending, premature death had interrupted them. And life went on for six years without incident.

The family moved back to Kate's native New York, this time settling in Port Jefferson. It was 1986. And Kate's evolution took a quantum leap.

CHAPTER FIVE

~∞~

Mellen-Thomas Benedict

The rental car was hardly visible as it traveled up a dusty dirt road that wound through the middle of an ancient Philippine rain forest. The driver and his passengers were surrounded by climbing palms with rough, spindly trunks and deep emerald saw-toothed fronds; by thick, twisted vines that clung to the trees; and by epiphytes, those strange archipelagic air plants that pulled moisture into their leaves. Survival of this variety was especially difficult now. It was the winter dry season and everything was brittle and dry, the mountain road seasonally dusty.

Fortunately, the driver knew the way. Mellen-Thomas Benedict had no idea how to find the village. A friend had suggested he spend a couple of days there while the film crew took a brief hiatus in Manila. All he knew was that the village was in the mountains, about fifty miles southwest of the capital.

"It's a holy mountain with caves where magic happens," his friend had told him. Apparently the mountain was just one of many extinct volcanoes on Luzon Island, the same place where Mellen's crew was going to be based for the duration of the filming.

He and the crew had arrived in the Philippines just four months before the presidential elections that Ferdinand Marcos had scheduled for February 1986. Expectation, mixed with apprehension, was almost palpable in the island country. After hammering through passage of a constitution that gave him an unlimited term, Marcos had finally relented to increasing pressure and agreed to new elections. His main opposition, Corazon Aquino, had virtually no experience, but she was extremely popular with the people. Many Filipinos feared Marcos would try to rig the election to deny Aquino a victory, and that this would lead to violence.

Nonetheless, Mellen had decided to go. He was in the Philippines to shoot a documentary about its psychic surgeons, shamans who appeared to perform surgery with their bare hands. He'd been able to get backing from a financier who was interested in psychic phenomena.

A lawyer friend from the old days in Atlanta— when Mellen was working on B movies—had shown him an amateur video documenting the surgeons' work. That was what got Mellen interested. He was fascinated. The footage showed the surgeons sinking their hands through patients' skin. They seemed able to open the skin, expose the bloodred tissue below, remove nodules and tumors, then seal the wound with their hands. Supposedly, the procedure was painless. Patients pronounced themselves cured. It seemed incredible.

This was precisely the kind of thing Mellen wanted to investigate. For years he'd worked on feature films in dusty Southwestern towns and in back lots around Atlanta, manning cameras and sound equipment or setting up dangerous stunts for car-crash movies and horror flicks. He'd found it engrossing for a while. The vagabond life didn't bother him. Nor did the thinness of the screenplays.

But then he'd begun to tire of it. After what had happened in 1982, his interests had shifted dramatically. He wanted to explore the spiritual dimensions of human life. If he could do it on film, all the better. When his friend told him about the psychic surgeons, he had to see for himself.

After a month in Manila and neighboring areas spent tracking down various surgeons, Mellen had come to the conclusion that a good number of them were fakes. They relied on sleight of hand, fake blood and bits of tissue hidden in their pockets. But even some of the fakes seemed to get results. Mellen chalked this up to the placebo effect. At the same time, however, he'd concluded that several of the surgeons he'd met and filmed were genuine.

This was especially true of one young, relatively unknown surgeon. Like most, he worked in a room in his house, a small shack with a thatched roof and usually a tabletop shrine to the Virgin Mary. A woman from Michigan was there when Mellen and his crew arrived. She was sitting in the cramped waiting room. She had a small growth behind her eye, a doctor back home had told her. It had been affecting her eyesight, and she was supposed to go in for surgery when she returned home. While in the Philippines, she decided to see a psychic surgeon. Mellen watched and the crew filmed as the surgeon called the growth out. A tiny fibrous mass of tissue emerged from behind the eye and fell to the table in front of the woman.

It was incredible, but Mellen had enough personal experience with the incredible not to dismiss something simply because it couldn't be explained by conventional standards.

After all, hadn't he died three years earlier of a brain tumor, only to come back to life after a fantastic journey through a sublime light? The brain tumor was nowhere to be found. "A spontaneous remission," his surgeon had declared it, scrutinizing Mellen's CT scan over a year later. Mellen wondered if it wasn't a miracle.

After what had happened in 1982 and all that had followed, Mellen was convinced there was more to the world than what could be seen and heard, touched and swallowed. One of the reasons he was interested in the psychic surgeons was that they appeared capable of the kind of inexplicable healing he'd experienced. And one of the reasons he was interested in going to the mountain was that he'd heard that many of the best psychic surgeons came from the region.

At the same time he was glad to escape Manila for a week. The city was crowded and noisy, ringed by miserable slums, dim terraces of plywood and cardboard shacks built on the edges of garbage dumps. A number of families might live in a single, rotting shack. Most upsetting was the children who would slip onto the narrow streets at night and call out to tourists staying in the whitewashed, luxury high-rise hotels that caught the breezes off Manila Bay. The little girls and boys would approach Mellen. Tall, with dark skin, brown hair and brown eyes, he was sometimes mistaken for a Filipino. But the way he dressed and got around in a rental car made it clear he was visiting from somewhere else and therefore had money.

When the rental car finally reached the village in the foothills of the mountain, Mellen was taken by how pleasant it was. Against a backdrop of terraced rice fields, surrounded by low stone walls, the village was a cluster of well-made, well-kept buildings. They were one story, with open windows and doorways, built of weathered timber with steeply sloped roofs thatched in palm leaves. The roofs stretched over deep porches in front and patios with flagstone floors in back. The village was hemmed in by a rain forest and shaded in the embrace of the mountain. The mountain was heavily wooded in spots and bright green at the base, where the dark soil had been terraced and planted with rice.

Mellen's driver, an American married to a Filipino, spoke both English and Tagalog. The driver would take him to see Anang, a shaman known as The Mother of the Mountain, he said. They would have to get Anang's permission to stay. The driver pointed out her house. It was similar to the others but a bit more spacious. She was home.

A small, frail woman with white hair worn short and loose, Anang came out to greet the group. The driver explained that they were here because they understood this mountain was a holy place and they wanted to learn more about it. Anang nodded and smiled, standing back from the visitors and considering them. But when she saw Mellen, she rushed forward.

"He is the patron saint of the mountain!" she announced, grasping Mellen's hand. "He has died and come back from the dead." She called several other villagers by name and ushered the group onto her porch. When everyone was assembled, she began to tell the story of Mellen's illness and death, his trip through the light, his return and what had followed, all with uncanny accuracy.

A few days later, Mellen found himself in the drafty cave of a middle-aged shaman, confronted with a question he wasn't able to answer immediately.

The group Anang had called to her home the first day of Mellen's visit consisted of shamans like herself, holy people. They had listened while Anang told the full story and then they had asked questions. Would Mellen bless some holy sites on the mountain? Would he stay and pray with them in their caves and write his name on the cave walls? Could he answer some questions?

"Did the Virgin Mary remain a virgin?" asked the middle-aged shaman, who looked very much like the other villagers, dressed as they were in worn but clean T-shirts and long pants. Still, there was an intensity about him that set him apart.

Mellen had spent six years at a Catholic boarding school in Vermont and should have known the answer. He was a student there from 1954 to 1960, kindergarten through fifth grade. His mother, Libby, had enrolled him and his brother, Michael, a year younger than he, after she divorced their father. A tall, striking woman with black hair, Mellen's mother had found work in the city as a runway model. Convinced New York wasn't a place to raise children alone, she sent daughter Elizabeth Anne to live with grandparents in Indiana and the boys to boarding school.

After six years at the school, Mellen should have known the answer to the shaman's question. But he'd never been particularly interested in Christian theology as a child, or in theology, period. He'd been fascinated by the Catholic conception of heaven and hell. The images the nuns described were both captivating and horrific. He'd become an altar boy. But that was more out of enjoyment of the ritual—the preparation of the altar, the ringing of the bells at the transformation of the host—than from an interest in the doctrine.

Dying changed a lot of things for him, though. After returning from the light to life three years earlier, he suddenly had access to information once beyond his ken. Mellen had a high school education; had worked for an advertising agency, then on feature films, finally in a stained-glass studio. Yet, to his own surprise, he was able to answer questions on a phenomenal range of subjects from global politics to quantum physics. Later, when he'd read about near-death experiences and the people who had been through them, he realized that others also had this ability. At the time, he wasn't sure why the information came to him. It simply did. Immediately after his return, he'd been able to hear the thoughts of those around him, and to feel their emotions as well. But this quickly became unbearable, and after a couple of years spent in near seclusion, he learned to tune out the voices.

Nonetheless, he continued to have access to information. He'd even invented a few things by using information gleaned from these trips into the light.

Standing in the shadow of the mountain now, he heard the answer to the shaman's question about the virgin and he repeated it.

"Mary was a virgin at Jesus' birth, but she got

dispensation to have other children after him," he told the shaman.

And the holy man was satisfied.

Over the next couple of days, other holy men asked Mellen to stay with them in their caves, write his name on the walls, answer questions. The caves were invariably dark and dank. At night, rats would eat the candles that were the sole source of light. Before the candles flickered out, Mellen would spot spiders as big as his hand lurking in crevices. It began to get a bit uncomfortable. Finally he asked to sleep on Anang's comfortable porch, which turned out to be the safest spot on the mountain.

All during his stay, even those nights in the caves, he had the most powerful dreams. They weren't dreams like most. They weren't dreams of events. They were dreams of purely emotional content. What he felt was love, an overwhelming love for people. He awoke elated.

The dreams were reminiscent of one part of his journey through the light.

At that point in the journey, he had been shown a whirling wheel of what he understood to be human souls. The wheel was made up of light, light of all colors. The bright images appeared and shifted and merged, as though viewed through a kaleidoscope. They were unspeakably beautiful. And Mellen understood this to mean that every soul was beautiful, capable of great love and compassion.

He was overcome by a love of mankind that he had never felt. Prior to his death and this trip through the light, he had come to regard people as the source of all that was wrong with the world, and capable of little that was worthwhile. All that changed after he returned from death.

The rest of the week Mellen stayed with Anang. They would get up at four-thirty each morning and sing prayers from a canon that was Roman Catholic but tinged with far more ancient beliefs. They'd sing until the sun came up. At any given time, someone in the village was singing prayers aloud. This lent a sacred quality to even the most mundane activities.

Toward the end of the visit, Anang called down from the mountain a shaman Mellen did not know. He'd heard that this man rarely left the cave where he spent his days in contemplation. When he appeared, Mellen was again overcome by a feeling of intense love, for this man and for all people. The shaman seemed to project this feeling. He stayed only briefly, returning to the mountain after hearing Mellen's story, blessing him and asking for a blessing from Mellen.

At the end of that week, the financier who had accompanied Mellen decided it was time to go back to Manila. "Get the driver and tell him to pack the car," he announced one morning. So Mellen told the driver and went to tell Anang.

"No, you can't go yet," she insisted.

"I've got to," Mellen explained. "He's taking the car." But Anang was adamant. "Something must happen first," she said.

As Mellen headed to the car, something did happen. He found it had two flat tires and no spare. There were no visible holes in the tires, but they were flat. Looking utterly defeated, the financier returned to Anang's porch and waited.

Anang then took Mellen inside a nearby house

in which the other shamans were waiting. They stood in line and asked him to bless them before he left. "You must bless me," he told them. And they did. No sooner had they finished than a small boy came by with a tire pump. Mellen pumped up the tires, helped load the car and got in.

As the car turned back down the dusty mountain road, he waved to the shamans and Anang, who had told him she had set aside a plot of land on the mountain for him. She asked him to return again to stay.

CHAPTER SIX

∽∾

Steve Price

American choppers leave Da Nang, gliding high above green-and-brown rice paddies. The air carries the stink of rotting jungle, chemically burned tropical forest contaminated by the deadliest defoliant on earth—Agent Orange. This is Vietnam during the American presence, and these smells mingle and mix with the distinct odor of napalm. These modern firebombs incinerate everything in their path, leaving a smell that sears its way clear through your head.

Knee-deep in dung-rich, muddied water below, rice farmers in Ho Chi Minh sandals made of discarded Goodyear tires look skyward into the rising sun. The spindling rice plants that surround them flap wildly from the windy gusts as choppers fly in formation across the countryside.

Like native dragonflies, these Huey helicopters hover together, then fly off in rapid succession toward targets on Marble Mountain just minutes away. A few months earlier, these brown-and-green camouflage-colored gunships might have flown up and down wide sections of the Connecticut River, near defense factories where they were built.

But that scene is ancient history and thousands of miles from Vietnam in the year 1968, when Marine Corps Staff Sergeant Steve Price returned in-country for a second tour. Price, a combat veteran now, is barely twenty-three years old and has already been decorated with the Purple Heart combat ribbon for the chest wound he survived three years earlier. Unshaven and dressed down in khaki fatigues, a floppy canvas hat and faded boots, Steve is armed with an M-16 rifle. It is the utility weapon of this war, the one most often carried by U.S. troops in this war. But Steve's weapon carried a special distinction that only its owner knew about for the year he spent in combat.

Choppers overhead are armed to repel, destroy and recover troops pinned down in tight swatches of jungle. This is Vietnam, where Huey helicopters are armored tanks, not just transport. These gunships ply treacherous jungle waterways between the South China Sea near China Beach and the River Tourane near the U.S. military facilities at Da Nang.

This is where Steve nearly died during his first tour, went into the light and survived. When he signed up for this second tour, he came in-country a changed man. But he did not know just how dramatic that change would be until he landed in Da Nang and got his orders and that M-16 rifle.

Flying in formation, the choppers head upriver toward military bases on Marble Mountain and China Beach. Below, the vista is permanently scarred by a thousand and one craters dug out by storms of five-hundred pound bombs as far as you can see. The earth is badly scorched; the stench is unforgettable. Soldiers sloshing through jungle and these rice fields never really know if they smell rotting vegetation or the thousands of decomposed bodies exposed to the jungle heat that cook men living or dead both day and night here.

This was no made-for-TV war, although battle scenes were played out nightly back home on the television news as if the war were some sort of daily television drama. It was an especially difficult war for Marines like Steve Price and Tommy Golden, whose units often took the brunt of combat assaults. This was what career men like Steve Price had trained for and were willing to give up their lives to do—kill the declared and undeclared enemies of the United States.

But killing also meant being killed, as Marine Corps veteran John Raths and others like him found out in a place called Cu Chi.

"They were throwing so much at us I couldn't believe it. We had flown in Wolfhounds [an elite infantry unit] to help us out," he said years later in a *Seattle Times* newspaper article. "They had gotten ahead of us and were taking very heavy fire. I got the order to pull back, but these three guys were pinned down behind an old French graveyard. I used the .50 Cal [machine gun] on an Armored Personnel Carrier [APC] to lay down a base of fire," said Raths. "I reached them and started to back out and ran out of ammunition. As soon as I stopped firing, one VC unloaded a whole clip." Raths got hit.

Bleeding badly, Raths slid down inside the personnel carrier. "My left lung had collapsed and I had four broken ribs and a sucking chest wound."

He, like Price, had returned to Vietnam a second time.

"One or two rounds tore out my spleen," he said, pointing to his body. "A few seconds later, I looked down and my intestines were blocking the hole in my gut. I couldn't understand the pain in my back. The thing that scared me the most was how hard it was to breathe," he reported.

Raths and the other wounded were evacuated out of the area on choppers.

"There was a black guy next to me on the helicopter; the whole lower half of his body was gone. They must have given him morphine or something, because he was smiling, saying, 'Hey, how you doing?' We clasped hands," Raths recalled.

When they arrived at the hospital, Raths overheard medics talking as they unloaded the wounded.

"Don't worry about that one," one of them said, looking at the black Marine. "He's dead. Get this one," the medic said, talking about Raths.

"They had to pry my hand out of his," Raths said.

This was the Vietnam Steve Price returned to after surviving his brush with death and one of the most incredible, peaceful experiences he had ever encountered. But Steve had also encountered a hellish revelation, one that would not be corrected for decades. It would be the single thing in his life that kept him always teetering on the brink of his own destruction. In this way he was much like Tommy Golden. But Steve would take a different path after years of self-destructive behavior that was really masking incredible pain.

To understand the kind of dedication Marines

like Steve Price showed by volunteering for second tours, you have to know that Vietnam was a hell-hole. The French first colonized the country in the 1950s. Then we arrived and continued the fighting for a dozen more years, which ended in a hastily planned withdrawal of U.S. troops in 1975. When Saigon fell, so did the facade of winning over the hearts and minds of Communists from the north. Nearly 10,000 villages disappeared during the war, more than half the hamlets in the country.

Our B-52 bombers thundered overhead day and night, pouring more explosive tonnage on this tiny country of thirty million people than in all of World War II.

While choppers bombarded enemy positions with rockets called in by the indigenous, paid look-outs stationed at the summit of Marble Mountain, enemy troops traversed a honeycomb network of caverns and man-made tunnels inside the same mountain.

The Vietcong operated a huge hospital in these caverns. Vietcong and regular North Vietnamese soldiers moved freely through this network, some-times dressing like local peasants by day who were friendly to Americans then launching deadly mor-tar and rocket attacks at night that maimed and killed teenage American boys sent over here to kill. This was how five-year-old Mai Lee was killed.

Out in the bush, an enemy lurked behind every clump of elephant grass and in any tree strong enough to hold a sniper. If a patrol wasn't am-bushed by roving bands of VC, unsuspecting men out on patrol could be struck down without warn-ing by one of the many deadly snakes that popu-lated this jungle country, or by booby traps laid by clever enemy troops.

VC commandos were just as deadly, equally as swift, flanking Marine Corps patrols by circling them, using a network of underground tunnels usually too small for our troops to find or explore. These same tunnels also led to and from any number of farming villages at the base of the mountain in a country where rice, not hamburgers, was the staple. Young Mai Lee was caught in this cross fire between our soldiers and enemy soldiers repelling what they considered invading interlopers like Steve Price.

An army on the run prized rice as a vital food cache for its stealth Vietcong and North Vietnamese regulars. Many of the battles fought at harvest time centered around huge rice crops and the military advantage American troops could have over a hungry enemy.

But just minutes away from Marble Mountain, GIs smoked free Lucky Strike or Camel cigarettes, ordered kegs and got to relax watching a churning surf roll up onto legendary China Beach. An elaborate recreation center for U.S. soldiers, complete with booze and five-dollar hookers, was set up right there on the same beach. The fenced-in resort was a haven for GIs coming out of the bush stinking from their own sweat and weeks without a real bath, unless you counted the soakings they sometimes got during the monsoons.

Downwind, but still along the vast shoreline of the South China Sea near the 17th parallel, the nose of a downed U.S. Navy A-6 Intruder aircraft lies buried in the sand. The plane is still loaded with five-hundred-pound bombs.

Thousands of American teenagers between the ages of sixteen and nineteen flew into the now famous Tan Son Nhut airport whole. Most left under far different circumstances. The war claimed more than 50,000 U.S. lives and untold numbers of Vietnamese. What is known about the casualties on their side is that an estimated 300,000 were missing in action.

After the war ended in 1975, our boys came home to an indifferent America and they were stung by the stigma of what would later be termed an unjust, undeclared war. We had left more than twenty-five million craters. What wasn't burned with incendiary devices like napalm was poisoned by the widespread spraying of deadly, toxic chemicals like Agent Orange.

This was Steve Price's war, the one in which he volunteered a second time after almost dying in battle. During a second tour, however, enemy soldiers had nothing to fear from this man from Connecticut, although looking at him would have betrayed any belief in that fact.

This was a brutal war, replete with all the horror related to any war. A film made by their side tells the eerie stories only those who had been there knew but couldn't always put into words. It begins with a scene of a drab Vietnamese army truck stopping at a mountain pass near Hanoi. The uniformed driver calmly lights a stick of incense. This is a ritual prayer for the souls he carries. The truck is packed with corpses stuffed in barrels and they are headed for burial at Trung Son, the largest cemetery for the war dead in Vietnam.

This is *Wild Reed*, the vision of director Vuong Taun Duc. The 1993 film depicts the fruitless trek by families along hundreds of miles of supply routes in the slim hope of finding the remains of their fallen sons. Tens of thousands were buried in mass, unmarked graves noted only on now faded paper maps.

"In the south you can sometimes see people walking in the road carrying a bag of bones," a Vietnamese journalist once told *Boston Globe* reporter Stan Grosfeld. The situation became so common after the war, federal laws were passed prohibiting bones on public buses, she said.

It was into this bloody war that Steve Price would step voluntarily for a second tour with Charley Company.

Once known as a bully from Deep River, Connecticut, this guy more closely resembled a biker on a Harley than the hero of the Corps he had become in just a few short years.

But Steve had all the markings of a real war hero.

Only heroes volunteered to serve a second combat tour, especially wounded veterans. A manly man even by Marine Corps standards, Steve weighed in at well over two hundred pounds. And just in case you had any doubts about that, he had covered himself with more than eighty daring tattoos. In military terms, Steve was a self-described lifer. The Corps trained its men to place the Corps' needs above all others, including wives and girlfriends. It might have been a cliché in the Army to say that if Uncle Sam wanted you to have a family, it would have issued you one. In the Corps, this was an unspoken gospel that every true leatherneck upheld.

Steve Price was willing to give up his life for the Corps. This dedication had almost cost him his life three years earlier, in 1965, after shards of hot shrapnel tore a hole in his chest and he started to die.

When Steve Price recovered he volunteered to

return to Vietnam in 1968. He carried his equipment off the plane to begin his second tour, wearing jungle gear like all the other Marine staff sergeants. He could walk the walk and talk shit like every swaggering lifer on that plane that morning.

But there was something different about Steve Price, something that even he did not know about himself until he stepped onto that runway and was heading for processing for incoming vets.

Yes, he knew he wasn't afraid to die, but didn't all Marines feel this way?

But not only did Steve Price no longer fear death. He could not kill either.

So he went through this war a second time, carrying an M-16 rifle he would not fire—not if his life depended upon it.

༄

CHAPTER SEVEN

Ken Ring

By 1975, Ken Ring had done the things he had wanted to do. He'd earned a Ph.D. in psychology, married the woman he hoped to marry and became the father of a bright ten-year-old. He was a tenured professor of psychology at the University of Connecticut, right there in old New England, where he'd set his southern Californian heart on living.

But something was missing. Now that all these things were finally attended to, he was caught unprepared by an overwhelming sense that something essential had been overlooked in the shuffle. He felt empty.

"I entered a time of sorrow and inward emptiness in my life," he would later say. "I remember feeling spiritually adrift, as if I had somehow lost my way. Suddenly, I found that I simply did not know what to do . . . the pervasive feeling of 'spiritual death' was continuing to paralyze me."

Thinking he might find some answers in the company of old people who could look back and reflect on their lives, he signed up as a volunteer at a nursing home that summer. The idea was, he'd go in and play cards with the residents. For Ken it was a ploy. He just wanted to hang out with old people and lead them into conversations about life.

But they just wanted to play cards. Their lives had hit dead ends in the retirement home, and they didn't want to think about it. When the summer ended, he didn't go back.

By chance one day that fall, Ken picked up Raymond Moody's book *Life After Life*. The book, which went on to become a surprise best-seller, was just out. It told the stories of people who, at the brink of death, had sublime experiences that were remarkably similar. Not only did they have these blissful experiences when they approached death, they seemed transformed when they came back to life. They felt renewed, had new purpose. They were excited by the possibilities in life, anxious to explore its limits. They rediscovered a sense of wonder and joy. They felt a renewed connection with, and love for, others.

Ken scribbled notes in the margins as he read.

Here are ordinary, average folks who seem to have these extraordinary experiences, he thought. If this is on the level, there must be more of them, and I could track them down and learn from them. The people who'd had these experiences seemed to achieve some higher state of consciousness, Ken thought. Maybe they had found answers to questions about the meaning of life, and other questions that people find answers to when they enter into those states.

Ken had always been interested in the study of alternate states of consciousness. He'd read about near-death experiences before and had been intrigued, in a professional sort of way. There were accounts of NDEs going back centuries. Plato had described one in his *Republic.* Albert Heim, a nineteenth-century Swiss geologist whose love of mountain climbing brought him close to death several times, spent twenty-five years collecting stories about near-death experiences. Moody's book reawakened Ken's interest in the subject. But this time it wasn't just a professional interest. It was personal as well.

Later that year, he convinced the university research foundation to finance a study. Ken had in mind a more scientific, systematic approach than Ray Moody had taken. The study was the first of many. One study would answer one set of questions. But inevitably it would raise others that had to be addressed in another study.

Nearly twenty years later, Ken still had questions. By then, he'd published three books about NDEs. He had established himself as a leading authority on the subject, sought after by scholars, experiencers, tabloid-talk-show hosts and legitimate journalists alike. He'd also established staid north central Connecticut—home to worldly Yankees and the U.S. insurance industry—as the incongruous heart of NDE country.

Dr. Bruce Greyson joined Ken there. A psychiatrist, Bruce had finished his residency at the University of Virginia and was staying on to work with the faculty there when Ray Moody arrived to start his residency. *Life After Life* was a best-seller by now, and Ray was getting hundreds of letters a day from NDEs who'd read the book and realized they'd gone through the same thing. But Ray was more interested in clinical psychiatry than research, so he turned the letters over to Bruce and Ian Stevenson, in the school's parapsychology division. That was how Bruce got interested.

His interest wasn't purely academic either. He saw a potential clinical application. NDEs appeared to take just a few minutes. But they changed people's lives permanently and profoundly. Even attempted suicides who'd had NDEs came back less suicidal. As a therapist, Bruce could work for years with a suicidal patient and see him make only incremental progress. Maybe there was a way to re-create some essential part of the NDE and use it in treatment, he thought.

From Virginia, Bruce took a detour to the University of Michigan. When Michigan turned a disapproving eye on his NDE research—the verdict was that the field wasn't "scientific enough"—he packed up for Connecticut.

The International Association for Near-Death Studies (IANDS) moved there too. Established by Ray, Ken, Bruce and several other NDE researchers, IANDS relocated to Ken's office, then settled a few towns away. The *Journal of Near-Death Studies* was launched there.

As the field of near-death studies became established, research papers also started appearing in mainstream professional publications like the *Journal of Nursing*. By 1994, IANDS had spun off hundreds of chapters and support groups in at least twenty-seven countries.

All this explains why, in the late 1970s, an inordinate number of people who had flirted with death were making their way to Connecticut.

They'd travel all the way from Ashtabula, Ohio, or Barcelona, Spain, or Rochester, New York, to participate in Ken Ring's and Bruce Greyson's studies. They wanted information themselves.

There were no support groups yet in Ashtabula, Barcelona, Rochester or anywhere else in the world. Connecticut became the place to go to. So Ken started putting them up. He converted a few rooms in his old house—originally built as an inn—into guest rooms and affectionately dubbed the place The Near-Death Hotel. All sorts of people checked in.

Tom Sawyer, a heavy-equipment operator from Rochester, was one.

Tom had been working under his truck one unexceptional morning in 1978 when the jack slipped and the pickup crushed his chest. He stopped breathing, then lost consciousness. And then something exceptional happened.

At that very moment he felt himself awakening. He awoke to complete darkness that slowly took the shape of a tunnel. At the end of the tunnel, far away, Tom could see a speck of white light. The light was the most beautiful thing he had ever seen. He felt himself moving faster and faster toward it. The moment he reached the light, he knew it was the all-encompassing light of God. Tom felt loved absolutely. He was able to ask the light questions—though he never spoke—and the answers came to him.

He asked whether there was an afterlife and understood that what he had come upon was a portal to the afterlife. He then saw his life literally pass before his eyes. He relived every moment, not just as himself, but as others who had been part of his life. He thought their thoughts and felt their feelings as well as his own. Afterward, he was given a choice. He could return to life or become part of the light. He chose to stay, but then suddenly felt himself reversing rapidly through the tunnel, slamming back down into his body.

"I'm the only person you'll meet who can say he was kicked out of heaven," Tom told Ken.

By then Ken had already found a pattern. Tom's experience, it turned out, was similar to many NDErs. Their experiences included several common elements. There was the out-of-body experience. Then came the trip through a tunnel toward a brilliant light that was identified both with the divine and with love. Then there was the passage into the light, accompanied by a blissful sensation of being loved and accepted unconditionally. Next came a life review that offered new insights because the NDEr experienced it as himself and as all the people who had been part of his life. Finally, there was a moment of choice when some were given an opportunity to stay or to return. Others were told to leave.

Basically, Ken's findings confirmed Ray's hypothesis—that near-death experiences had certain elements in common. But Ken and Bruce found there were variations on the theme, depending on how people nearly died.

If you attempted suicide, you didn't have it as good as you did if you nearly died from an illness or accident. Suicides tended to have truncated experiences that ended before they reached or even noticed the light at the end of the tunnel. While in the darkness, though, most were able to understand that suicide was wrong. They were left with the message that life did have a purpose and that they were going to be sent back because they had something to do.

Whether you went to church or synagogue, believed in God or life after death, didn't seem to make you any more or less likely to have an NDE. Not everyone who was near death had a near-death experience. The odds of having one were about forty percent, as best Ken could figure.

But religious beliefs could affect one element of the experience: the entrance into the light. Christians were more likely to say they encountered Jesus in the light, while Hindus were more apt to meet a deceased relative or messenger of Krishna; and Buddhists, to see the Buddha. Nonetheless, most came back believing that all religions were equally valid.

"It doesn't matter what church I belong to because God is in all of them," they'd say.

If you'd been drugged or delirious when you neared death, you were likely to have no NDE at all. And if you knew about NDEs before you nearly died, you were also more likely to miss out on the experience.

But people unlucky enough to nearly die under anesthesia or after head injuries could have it even worse. These people were the only ones who reported a significant number of hellish NDEs. It turned out there were such things. These were trips to lands of fiery lakes and demons. There was no happy ending in a sublime light. Even more chilling, there were NDEs that turned out to be travels to nothingness. Returning, people would say they'd found themselves suspended in emptiness with nothing to see or hear or contemplate but the horrible suspicion that life ultimately went nowhere. Both types of experiences seemed to be rare.

Phenomenal as the experiences themselves were, Ken found that the transformations that followed could be even more compelling.

"Why don't you ask us questions about how our

lives changed after our NDEs?" Helen Nelson had
suggested.

Helen was one of the first NDErs Ken interviewed and she became a close friend. In her mid-
thirties, she'd had a profound NDE during surgery.
She left her body behind and traveled to a beautiful
crystalline valley. It was an otherworldly place illuminated by a brilliant but soothing light. Helen
felt perfectly calm there and wandered a while
through the valley until she met a man she was
later able to identify as her late grandfather. Helen
had never seen him before, but she recognized him
in an old family photo after she returned.

"Helen, don't give up," her grandfather had told
her. "You're still needed. I'm not ready for you
yet."

The NDE was a rebirth, an awakening, Helen
told Ken. After the experience, she had more con-
fidence in herself. She felt she could do anything.
She had a greater interest in spirituality and was
certain there was a God. She lost all fear of death
and lived her life with more relish.

Ken took her suggestion, quizzing other NDErs
about changes in their lives, and found a pattern
again. NDErs reported similar changes in their
lives after their experiences. They came back un-
afraid of death and certain of an afterlife. They appreciated life and themselves more. They had a
higher self-esteem. They showed greater compassion and concern for other people. They were less
interested in material success and more interested
in spiritual enrichment.

It seemed the NDE was therapeutic. People who
had been batted around in life were patched up. In
the light, they felt unconditionally loved and accepted, sometimes for the first time. They felt part

of the light and realized that they, and everyone else, were all parts of the same whole. The life review also seemed to have a healing effect. Reliving scenes from their lives as the other people who had been taking part, NDErs understood things that had always escaped them.

That made all the difference for Barbara Harris.

A Michigan housewife, Barbara had always suffered from low self-esteem. She'd always believed herself a bad and unworthy kid—she was often in hot water with her parents—and carried these feelings of low self-worth with her to adulthood. When she was thirty-two, she had an NDE after back surgery. Reviewing her life from the vantage point of the others who'd been part of it, Barbara understood for the first time why her mother had been so distant and her father so harsh when she was a child. She realized she'd been neither bad nor undeserving as a child, or as an adult, for that matter. After the NDE, she was able to respect and love herself.

The life review also seemed to teach people an extraordinary empathy for others. It made sense, of course. Not only did they relive scenes from their lives as themselves, they went through it all again as all the others who'd shared their lives. Moreover, the life review usually played back a certain kind of scene, one in which the NDEr helped another person, or passed up the opportunity to help someone in need.

A rough customer who would just as soon throw a punch as argue, Tom Sawyer found himself on the receiving end of his life review. Smack in the middle of the review, he found himself speeding through the streets of upstate New York again. This was the day he'd cut off another driver, the man had objected and they fought. Tom left the man unconscious on the pavement and roared off in his car. That was how it all felt again when he relived the scene as himself. But, simultaneously, he also went through it as the other guy. He experienced the beating he gave the man, each and every blow, thirty-two punches in all, until he himself fell unconscious to the pavement. After the NDE, Tom gave up fighting and speeding and the rough life in general.

However, the road from before to after was rockier than Ray's book had suggested, Ken discovered. People were transformed, but often only after a very, very tough transition period. Some, like Tommy Golden, who finally succeeded with his suicide in the cemetery that day, just didn't make it.

There were some obvious reasons the transition was tough. Having identified and empathized so completely with others, many NDErs found it impossible to carry on as though it were every man for himself. Hard-nosed businessmen and journalists couldn't stomach the competition any longer. Policemen, organized-crime figures and soldiers like Steve Price couldn't fire their guns anymore. Careers foundered.

So did relationships. "I used to think before this that I really loved my spouse. But in part it was possessiveness, part yearning, part security and part sexuality. It wasn't unconditional love and now I feel that for everyone," one man told Ken after his NDE.

That kind of thing made it hard for spouses to relate. While Tom's wife liked the kinder, gentler guy who came home from the hospital, she wasn't so happy to find that he would go off without a minute's notice to help perfect strangers, even when there was plenty that needed to be done at home.

A Mafia bagman who left a crime family after his NDE was later abandoned by his girlfriend because he wasn't interested in making money anymore. She still wanted the kind of good time that didn't come cheap.

And Barbara Harris ultimately left her husband. The wealthy wife of a Michigan auto executive, Barbara had been married for years when she had her NDE. She and her husband had always enjoyed the things money could buy—their Bloomfield Hills home, a private plane, expensive cars, lavish parties and vacations. In 1976, the couple flew their plane to Washington as a personal way of celebrating the nation's bicentennial. These goodies and their three children were the things that held them together.

After Barbara had her NDE, though, the big house, the cars, the plane, the parties and the vacations lost their luster. She took a trip to meet Ken, stayed at The Near-Death Hotel, then moved to Connecticut permanently. She wanted a life that was more spiritually fulfilling, and for starters, she wanted to understand what had happened to her at the edge of death. Her husband's interests and her own weren't the same anymore. They divorced and she took a poorly paying job at the University of Connecticut to do research, help run IANDS and attend the support group meetings. The changes in her life came at great sacrifice. Barbara couldn't support the children, who stayed with their father.

In the end, she sorted it out, figured out what she wanted to do, discovered a rewarding career as a writer and speaker and found a way to spend time with her children. But it was no cakewalk.

And some NDErs found the way even harder. A number turned to drinking and drugs. There was one boy who'd had an NDE when he was fourteen. He'd been electrocuted in a freak accident and had an experience that was both heavenly and hellish. He'd found himself walking down a path through a crowd. On one side were demons; on the other, heavenly beings. At the end of the path, Jesus welcomed him, but explained it wasn't his time to die.

"I was sent back by Jesus to do something important," he told his mother in the hospital recovery room. But he was still just a kid in high school. He wasn't in any position to save the world. He still had to pass Geometry and American History. Depressed and frustrated, he started drinking, then experimenting with cocaine, and finally became suicidal. His mother took him to Bruce, who counseled him and introduced him to the IANDS support group.

Whether things worked out depended on a lot of variables, Ken concluded. The way other people responded, whether they were receptive or not, was one. A lot of NDErs found the support group helpful.

And there were other variables. NDErs who sought out information that helped them understand their experience, as Barbara did, generally fared better. People like Mellen who steered clear of friends who didn't share their new values also had it easier in the end. Sometimes the right job made all the difference. A good number of NDErs found happiness as teachers and clergymen and health-care workers. The boy who had the NDE at fourteen found some peace of mind as an emergency medical technician.

In the end, their transformations were what convinced Ken and Bruce that NDEs were something unique and very real, not just vivid dreams or hallucinations or delusions, as the skeptics and debunkers would have it.

There were plenty of skeptics. At the university, Ken still caught flak from colleagues almost twenty years after he'd taken the plunge into NDE studies, even though the field had gained credibility—thanks in large part to his work. He kept his eye on the humor in his situation.

"My early sensitivities to the professional costs of stepping over the boundaries of accepted scholarly concerns never entirely eroded," he wrote in the preface to his third book, *The Omega Project*, in 1992. "Even to innocent undergraduates who, knowing my reputation for the exotica of psychology, would sometimes approach me to sponsor their academically dubious projects, I would joke, 'Look, even I have my limits, and I don't do ghosts and I don't do UFOs, so don't even ask me to consider it!' "

The way the debunkers told it, the NDEs that Ken had made his lifework were either dreams or hallucinations or delusions. That was it. If not that, the experiences were simply the result of an insufficient supply of oxygen to the brain, or they were brought about by an excess of endorphins, natural pain killers. Everyone knew the body produced endorphins at times of crisis. Apparently they could also prompt the mind to conjure up images of salvation to stave off the trauma of impending death, it was argued.

But both Ken and Bruce knew hallucinations and endorphin surges and the like didn't bring about the kind of transformations they saw in NDErs. And hallucinations and surges couldn't account for Kate's sudden talent as a painter, or Mellen's knack for invention, or Tom's ability to understand quantum physics.

That had been another strange thing. Tom had a high school education and hadn't picked up a book on his own since seventh grade. But soon after his NDE, he began scribbling down complex mathematical equations and passages from books about quantum physics. When he went to the library to check out a few books on the subject—no walk in the park—he understood them intuitively. Eventually, he enrolled in college.

And then there were the strange electromagnetic effects. Everyone, every living thing, generated an electromagnetic field. But some NDErs seemed to come back with something different about theirs. Some NDErs couldn't walk down the road without making all the bulbs in the streetlights overhead fizzle out. Others couldn't touch a stereo or tape recorder without leaving it on the blink. And then there were Mellen and Kate and Barbara, who seemed to generate fields that calmed and maybe even healed people who got close to them. Endorphin surges didn't seem an adequate explanation.

After nearly twenty years, Ken still isn't sure what happens during an NDE. He's not sure whether it's mystical or neurological.

He suspects, though, that it's both.

The way he sees it, NDErs are getting a glimpse of truth itself. The truth is that the light and all that's connected to it—which is everything—make up a whole. Love holds it all together.

Most people don't see this in their workaday lives, he says. Their sense of separateness—their egos—gets in the way.

But near death, the senses shut down and

breathing is disrupted. All the physiological and psychological supports for the ego crumble. For the first time, people get to see through the ego and glimpse the truth.

This could explain why NDErs return understanding the ins and outs of, say, biochemistry when they've never studied a chemical reaction, Ken figures. If the light includes everything, it includes an understanding of all knowledge, and gives NDErs access to it.

Some neurologists believe there's a flash of neurological firings in the brain near death. If so, Ken speculates, this barrage of firings could rewire the brain, allowing NDErs to make use of more than just the tiny fraction of the human brain that most of us use. And that, he says, could explain why NDErs return with talents that once went unrecognized.

Whatever happens, Ken is certain the experiences change people profoundly.

They've changed him, he says.

When he first started interviewing NDErs, he felt it. It was as though he were vicariously going through some of what they'd gone through. The lessons they'd learned from their experiences, the stories they told, resonated. The effect was almost immediate.

Their message was so refreshingly simple: love one another more.

"I found that I was no longer oppressed by the spiritual deadness that had, ironically, provided the initial impetus to my research," Ken wrote in the preface to his first book, *Life at Death*. "In fact, my feeling was becoming just the opposite."

Everyone, Ken believes, can benefit from the experiences people like Kathy and Steve and Kate and Mellen have gone through. NDErs, he says, are advanced scouts, who come back to teach us all something. Simply by hearing their stories, he says, we change.

CHAPTER EIGHT

᭦

Kathy Latrelle

Early in her marriage to Alan, Kathy didn't think about what had happened in Waterbury. Things seemed to be going smoothly. Though happy, she still found it hard to relax and not worry.

She'd met Alan at Ehrling Bergquist Regional Air Force Hospital in Omaha. They were both twenty, both in the Air Force. She was an X-ray technician at the hospital. He was a medic.

Kathy had been sent to Omaha after basic training at Lackland Air Force Base, a sprawling command in San Antonio. In basic training, she met Maggie, the first friend she'd made since childhood. Kathy still felt uncomfortable around other people.

My social skills are garbage, she thought when she compared herself to Maggie, who seemed particularly adept with people. Kathy didn't feel uncomfortable around Maggie, though. Maggie had the much rarer knack and desire to make other people feel at ease.

Alan arrived in Omaha from Rock Island, Illinois, a mill town. His father was a welder. Alan might have been a welder too, if he hadn't enlisted in the Air Force.

Kathy noticed Alan in the operating room at Ehrling right off. She worked down the hall in X-ray. "My God! He's beautiful. A forty-six-inch chest. A thirty-one-inch waist," she later wrote Maggie, who had gone to a base in California.

And Alan was a great stitcher, the best Kathy had ever seen. He could sew up a dog-eared flesh wound so there'd be no trace of a scar. Alan had noticed Kathy too. She was funny and scrappy. He liked that.

He started telling her jokes in the hospital. She liked his sense of humor. Often it had an edge to it, a certain anger, like her own; below the surface, they were both angry.

Alan's childhood had been similar to Kathy's in some respects. His father had been tough. Alan's mother was terrified by him.

Anger was one of the things Kathy and Alan had in common, for a while at least. They both had short fuses. Kathy never lost her temper on the job; she knew that would create problems. But she was certain her commanding officer sensed same defiance in her, and she was certain that was why she never got promoted.

"I was an angry young woman," she once told Ken Ring. After she nearly died, the anger disappeared. "I think Alan liked me a little better when I was angry."

Alan and Kathy started seeing each other soon after they met. They went to movies; listened to the Beatles, the Beach Boys and Uriah Heap on the stereo. They went bowling. Alan would stop by the house where she was keeping her motorcycle and watch her work on it.

They got married five months later. It was May 1974. Kathy felt almost light-headed, she was so happy. She was certain no one had ever been as deeply in love as she and Alan. They moved into a house off-base. Kathy loved dogs, and over time, they salvaged two mutts from the pound, a Welsh Border collie mix named Stripe and a shepherd-collie named Toofer. She was Kathy's favorite, and the reason, ultimately, Kathy decided not to die.

She and Alan didn't intend to have any children; neither of them liked spending time around kids. They irritated her, got on her already jangly nerves, and she had other things to do.

The first year or so was happy enough. She and Alan both worked long hours, Alan in particular. After finishing her fourth year in the Air Force in 1976, Kathy decided not to reenlist. Instead, she took a job as an X-ray tech at the University of Nebraska Medical Center in Omaha. Alan signed on for another hitch. As was usually the case in the service, he worked a lot of overtime.

They were working different shifts and some days didn't see each other at all. He'd come in exhausted at 3 A.M. and she'd head off to work five hours later. She didn't mind. Kathy liked having the time to herself to read and work on the motorcycle. She'd even do a minimal amount of cleaning, which she hated.

But Alan minded. He minded that she was so independent and that she didn't need him around more. She could see it was bothering him more and more.

*   *   *

But Kathy had long been used to being alone. When she was fifteen her mother finally threw her father out of the house. After five years of breakdowns, her mother couldn't stand the strain. Her father had stopped working. He stopped showing up for accordion lessons, couldn't finish a performance. People stopped calling him. Except for the violent outbursts, it was as if he weren't there at all.

And by then, her mother had already met Ted. He was a guard at Connecticut Valley, a big, burly guy with curly black hair and brown eyes. His job was to keep the patients in line, and if that meant smacking them around, that was what he did.

So when Kathy was fifteen, she and her mother moved out of the house in Woodville and into an apartment in a seedy section of downtown where they worried about getting mugged at night. Her father rented a place in a hotel downtown. When Lloyd came back on leave, he stayed with their father.

Kathy's mother started spending more time at Ted's house in Middlefield, about three-quarters of an hour north of her apartment. She'd work nights at Waterbury Hospital, stop by the apartment to pick up dirty laundry and drop off groceries for Kathy, then head over to Ted's house. Often she'd call up late at night and say, "I'm not coming home tonight, Kathy, okay?" Kathy would spend another evening alone.

Kathy felt abandoned by her father, by Lloyd, by her mother. But she never confided in anyone. Even when her mother was around, they never spoke much. And when they did speak, they often argued. "Don't you tell me what to do. You don't sleep here!" Kathy exploded one night when her mother told her to wash a teetering pile of dishes in the sink. She was far more hurt than angry.

After a year of the late-night calls, her mother moved in with Ted—alone. Kathy wasn't welcome. When angry, she never minced words. She'd already honed a sharp tongue for those occasions.

"A drunken, womanizing asshole who hits my mother and treats her like dog shit,' " she'd called Ted. Of course, he was some of those things. He'd racked up several cars while driving drunk. And he had a roving eye. But he didn't like hearing about it, particularly from Kathy. As far as he was concerned, she was a hellion with a bad mouth. She wasn't welcome in his house. Ted never realized how rejected and afraid she felt. On those occasions she kept her feelings to herself, covered them over with sarcastic remarks.

The problem, as far as Alan was concerned, was that Kathy was too independent.

Kathy knew that all the women in Alan's family were extremely dependent. "His family is a kind of backwoods farm family where the men are men and the women are scared," she told a friend.

Kathy had stopped depending on people a long time ago. No one she'd crossed paths with had been particularly dependable. She had her job, her motorcycle, her books. And she had Alan. She didn't want to rely on him alone. After all, what if he disappeared one day?

She had reason to worry. One afternoon a few months earlier, Alan had told her he'd been offered an assignment in Turkey—unaccompanied. She knew he didn't have to accept the assignment. She also knew he might. After all, he could have turned it down immediately. Kathy knew she was sup-

posed to plead with Alan, beg him to refuse the
orders. But she wouldn't. She didn't even have to
talk about it. The tension between them continued
to escalate.

One night shortly before their fourth anniver-
sary, Alan came home in a particularly bad mood.

"I took the orders to Turkey," he said abruptly.

My God! Kathy thought. He actually did it? He's
leaving. What am I going to do? I'm going to be
here all alone. I can't. I really can't live without
him.

But she didn't say any of those things.

"You stupid fool! What do you think you're doing? You creep!" she said. And that was the end of
it.

An uncomfortable month and a half later, Alan
finally left. He packed a few bags, boarded a plane
and was gone. After that, Kathy lived alone for six
months with just the dogs for company. By then,
she heard her father was dying of lung cancer.

Her father had gone to the Veterans Administra-
tion hospital feeling lousy. The doctors there diagnosed the cancer, and something else. He had a
thyroid problem, they told him. When he'd had his
thyroid removed, back when Kathy was ten, he
should have started taking thyroid medication. No
one in the family had given a second thought to
the operation after it was over. But now, fourteen
years later, the doctors were saying that the lack of
thyroid hormone was to blame for his bizarre
mood swings, the weeks of depression and lassi-
tude, and the bouts of mania. Thyroid hormone
would have smoothed that right out, they said.
And it did. After he took his first dose, he never
had another breakdown.

Kathy was stunned. What a waste! What a cruel

joke! Now that her father was finally all right, he was going to die. She began writing and calling him, and they started to straighten things out.

She realized she missed him and she had to admit she even missed her mother. Things had changed for the better with her mother as well, now that they were out of each other's shadows.

With no reason to stay in Omaha, and with nowhere else to go, she decided to return to Waterbury. Just six years earlier, she'd been sure she was escaping once and for all. Now she was going back, back to the brass mills and the Knights of Columbus clubhouses.

On one of the hottest June days Kathy could remember, Ted flew out to Nebraska to help her move. She and Alan owned two cars and she needed somebody to drive one back East. Ted helped her pack, something she never expected him to do. Early in the afternoon, they pulled out of her driveway in Omaha and began the long trip back to Waterbury, Connecticut.

〰

CHAPTER NINE

Kate Valentine

Raised Irish Catholic in the 1950s, Kate had always been able to escape into books. In a family with four girls, Kate always felt like an orphan and would jokingly tell people later in her life that she had been born into the wrong family.

Though her favorite stories had been those of Shakespeare, she preferred any world where she could escape the beatings and verbal abuse she suffered as a girl at home in Northport, the Long Island, New York, community where her carpenter father had settled the family.

A withdrawn and solitary child, Kate also like to soothe herself with classical music, easily found on the radio in her room that could get any one of the many sophisticated programs in nearby Manhattan. While Kate listened to WQXR broadcast live performances from Carnegie Hall, her father listened to the earthy twang of country-and-western music while he drank in the next room.

These seemingly highbrow takes clearly put her at odds with her alcoholic, immigrant parents. Drinking Irish weren't stereotypes: they were real to Kate, who noticed other peculiar things about the family. Her mother, for example, hung dime-store art two inches from the ceiling anywhere in the house, and she rarely read. And when she did, it would have been *Newsday*, the Long Island daily, not the sonnets that Kate preferred.

But it wasn't just her parents whom Kate felt this alienation from. Other relatives, like her aunts and her father's four brothers, also had similar reputations with this child. In fact, other people must have viewed them as a strange clan too, because, Kate says, outside of family members, her parents had no friends. It was partly because of the way they drank and carried on. Her father could fly into rages without warning, sending Kate and her sisters scurrying to the safety of their rooms. Her mother, a housewife, sank into the silent routine typical of alcoholic families, in which dysfunction and chaos become the only true family traditions.

Describing herself as a strange child, Kate knew how to read at four, and at five, learned to read Shakespeare. While the world's most sophisticated city was just minutes away on the Long Island Expressway, Kate was trapped in Northport in a family of drinking men, abused and abusive women.

One of four sisters, Kate always felt like the daughter most easily forgotten. She could easily slink away silently into her books, since it was easier to witness the difficulties of young Hamlet or King Lear than to face her boisterous uncles and aunts, whose punishments could sometimes border on the cruel and unusual, especially to a small child unable to fend them off. To be seen and heard meant risking being hurt in some instances in this family, and retreating was more than a quirk. It meant survival.

Kate can still remember the time her father was in the hospital and these aunts came over to take care of her. She was only about three years old, but this memory stuck like an indelible tattoo.

While Kate couldn't remember what crime she had committed, she would forever remember the punishment—they threatened to burn her alive.

The family lived in an old house that had grates covering a heating duct leading to an open coal-burning furnace in the basement. Scolding her for something, the aunts suddenly picked up one of the grates and tossed it aside. They grabbed Kate's hands and legs and held her body over the open flames, threatening to thrown her into the fire below unless she behaved.

"I was only three or four, but I remember it clearly," she said. "These were angry people and they loved the power and feelings that come with that anger. These people were nutso; they didn't have any friends. They had their families and they were all the same," she recalled.

School became Kate's refuge.

"I thought I'd died and gone to heaven," said this woman who had cried when her parents wouldn't send her to summer school. At home, where her mother cleaned house, made beds and spent all day tending to the needs of the family, Kate could never really hide from her father's uncontrollable outbursts and fits of rage.

"I tried to always please them. You were always afraid you would trigger his anger," she said, betraying no emotion saying this now as an adult. "If the salt wasn't on the table, you got beat for it.

"I think he drank to medicate himself," she said, making an observation she could not have absorbed or understood as a child. "He had four brothers and they were the same. This kind of behavior went back forever in his family.

"He listened to music like 'Don't Shoot the Bartender, He's Half Shot Now'," she said in a mocking way as baroque music drifted through her orderly painting studio near her home in Connecticut.

These were the memories of a woman who had come a long way.

By 1994, Kate had moved to one of the many affluent towns in upper Fairfield County, the Connecticut gold coast. Ironically, the sleepy place she chose resembles a Norman Rockwell painting. But it is just south of Waterbury, where Kathy Latrelle's story began.

By contrast, Kate Valentine's little town is an American classic that includes a central Main Street, a greengrocer who knows customers by their first name, little boutiques and other throwbacks in time.

The town, which will remain anonymous to protect Kate's need for more privacy now, is itself quietly famous. It has a world-renowned reputation for high-quality antique stores and old-world artifacts that range from paintings and sculpture to farming Americana. It is also home to craftsmen, retouchers and refinishers whose fields cover every kind of collectible, especially furniture pieces from various styles and periods. The town attracts an assortment of highly skilled people who do museum-quality restorations and prepare auctionable pieces on consignment or commission.

Kate settled in among them a few years after her NDE and quietly began sharing a gift she only discovered she had by struggling to understand what had happened to her the night she died.

*   *   *

Kate Valentine had been a type A personality. She would have been the type featured on a *Money* magazine cover story about "having it all." Kate wanted her children to go to the right schools, to meet the right children so that they would marry the right people. They had always lived in the right parts of town, driven the right cars and attended the right churches until her NDE.

A son who moved to Florida and married someone his mother had not approved of first, became a successful and happy car salesman. This decision would have triggered a real death experience in his mother before her life changed, before her NDE. This woman, who says she would never have survived this son's decision prior to her experience in the light, now says she is simply delighted that he is happily married, has children and is doing what he wants to do. Sometimes these transformations appear to be just that simple. People like Kate say the experience taught them to love other people unconditionally—something she could never do in the past.

Along the path to learning this seemingly simple lesson, Kate had to let go of ways that had become second nature to her, she says. Money and its power were among the first material lessons Kate had to learn. After her illness and recovery, she and Paul were suddenly plagued by serious financial problems that eventually led to bankruptcy.

"We lost everything," Kate said years later, "the house, the cars, everything, and I had to clean offices and do other jobs to pay our bills." The experience became part of a broadening shift in values she says made her appreciate the things she did have.

"I learned to trust. We learned that we would get the things we needed when we needed them." Then she tells the story of the missing rent money, one of the many parables in her new and changing life.

The rent was due, $725, and the Valentines didn't have it. Their teenage daughter came home and offered to lend them the money from an account Kate was sure had no more than fifty dollars in it. But, needing even that small amount, Kate drove to the bank, still not knowing where she was going to find the rest of the money.

"We told the teller we wanted to close this account," she said, "and the teller handed my daughter exactly seven hundred and twenty-five dollars. This was just one of the many times this kind of thing has happened to us."

Back at home, she told Paul the story and they both knew they had again experienced one of those small, unexplained miracles you expect to hear about only in television movies. Kate would later become the CEO for a branch of the YMCA. Their financial problems dissolved.

"There was this little flame that started flickering with the NDE," she would later claim. "I had just begun to fan it from time to time and things began happening."

After her NDE, she stepped off a fast track which she had fought so hard to find. She no longer cared about the cars she drove or the houses they bought or sold. The pendulum of her life slowed and so did the pace of her own inner clock, she said. Kate was in the swing of a full-blown spiritual shift and it was rocking the foundations of her beliefs, one belief at a time.

As she was able to turn her thoughts inward more and more, and as she did, she discovered she could retrieve knowledge and skills that had previously gone undetected and unused.

Unable to draw even the most basic of objects like fruit or vegetables, she had once taken art lessons with Paul. But Paul later confided that she was hopelessly artless. After her NDE, however, this limitation gave way to an ability that has allowed her to become a full-time artist and teacher.

Kate specializes in painting art objects in the simple style of eighteenth-century decorative artists. She commissions her builder husband to build replicas of period furniture pieces, on which she and her students paint scenes and landscapes. Among the many paintings that decorate her small studio are vivid scenes of rolling green hills and valleys.

This new career grew out of a poorly executed hobby begun when Kate first fell ill. She never took any formal art lessons after she and Paul had tried it, because she had shown almost no aptitude. After her NDE, however, she took six lessons to learn how to mix paints and colors, but not how to draw or paint. On her own, she began to use painting techniques she later learned were in the style of unnamed eighteenth-century artists whom her period scenes apparently mimicked.

What led her to this town and this uncharacteristic life as a painter began eight years earlier, after the NDE.

"We have to go back to that night when I expected to die," she says. "I can't explain how I got well. I came back from this experience and I was healed. I had what I called a dream back then. I had been fighting to stay alive long enough to take care of those things you have to tidy up, and I don't think you die until you say okay."

And that night she had given in, certain she would die. Instead, she first found herself in an intensely dark place, then saw a burst of light that enveloped her.

"It was a transition so sudden, I was overwhelmed by the colors I saw. It was so peaceful, I felt relieved, and it was like coming home," she said, clearly lost in the memory of this experience again as she talked.

Looking around her studio, crowded with paintings on antique replicas of chiming clocks, tables and wooden boxes, visitors ask Kate to hear her story again. In the background, Aaron Copland's *Appalachian Spring* plays softly.

"What I experienced was this all-pervasive darkness," she says, "not a tunnel. And then there was this burst of light. It was the brightest thing I had ever witnessed, but it wasn't blinding. I was standing on these incredibly high mountains, looking down into these valleys. We only bring back that which is significant," she says, talking about her experience.

"What is the significance of the valleys in your experience?" one of the visitors asks as he pours cream into his Styrofoam cup.

"Oh, I think metaphorically, I think the valleys might have meant that I could have stayed in that beautiful place had I gone down into those valleys." Her visitors look around the room. The same mountains and valleys Kate has just described clearly seem to be depicted in painting after painting hanging in the studio.

"So this is why you paint your NDE over and over again?" she is asked.

Kate is visibly stunned by the question. "I didn't realize I had been painting any of it in my work," she replies after a long pause in what had been a free-wheeling conversation. There's a silence, not an awkward one, while she clearly views her work in a new light, considering the question she has just been asked.

"This and other things like it happen on an unconscious level," she says, appearing ready to get into a philosophical explanation. But something stops her.

"I keep telling other people to keep things simple. I don't know why I am so surprised at all of this. I didn't think I was painting the experience, but now that you mentioned it, I guess I have been painting some part of it over and over again.

"A woman came to me and said she was having a problem praying. She wanted to pray but was having problems getting started." Kate launches into another story to clear the air. "I told the woman to make two cups of tea, one for herself, one for God. When you get the tea made, sit down and talk to God as if you had invited a friend over for tea. That's how simple all of this really is," Kate says.

"So, why do you paint the scenes from your NDE over and over?" her visitor asked again.

"Because they're in my head. They're simple and maybe they're what I saw in my NDE. I can't forget the vivid colors I saw that night, and maybe, just maybe, I keep painting the same scene over and over again, trying to capture those colors. The colors in this reality are like the reverse side of a tapestry you know," she tells her visitors.

* * *

But Kate didn't always tell her story. It took her more than six years before she could tell anyone, including her husband, Paul. She told it for the first time one day in 1986, to a nurse named Ellen who lived near the Valentines when they were living in Port Jefferson, New York.

After her NDE, Kate had resumed living what you might call a routine life. After seeing her doctors, who could only confirm that she was in remission, Kate just got stronger and stronger.

Life went on.

It had been six years since her miraculous remission back in Connecticut. While she thought about what had happened, knew it was mystical in some way, it still didn't consume every minute of her days or nights. She was raising her family, after all, children she had never expected to see grown up. Paul had his Kate back after some sort of fluke, a quirky but explainable fluke. But *they* couldn't explain it, that was all.

So they resumed their life together.

Kate, had always been the consummate woman in control. She was practical and liked control. She took care of everything, wielding her control like a silent sword. She knew that what she had experienced wasn't in the realm of rational, conventional science. Without that kind of proof, she could be labeled a kook. She had also come from a family in which it had always been noble to suffer in silence.

So she told no one, not even Paul, what she knew about her recovery. It had been no mystery to her because she was informed during the experience and had learned many unfathomable things in it.

But the silence was all washed aside one morning when a friend named Ellen dropped by for coffee. As Kate poured Ellen a cup, the nurse started talking about a patient who had just been revived after nearly dying. Ellen said the patient reported having a near-death experience and had seen beautiful hills. Then she described scenes of beautiful rolling hills, a peaceful, guiding light and valleys similar to those Kate had seen. Kate, who had not taken up art at this time, could see the lush panorama in her mind's eye and knew it.

Excited, she dropped her long cloak of secrecy and told her story for the first time.

She also began writing a manuscript that finally ballooned into a two-hundred-page autobiography.

This is my therapy, Kate told herself as she wrote, sometimes late into the night. The more she wrote, the more peaceful she seemed to feel. She was becoming happier, less worried about things. Something had fallen away and was replaced with a lightness that Paul secretly worried about. He thought his wife had taken a lover.

As she wrote, astounding information just seemed to flow to her. It was basic at first, like being able to remember long-forgotten details in stories about her family just when she needed them for the book. Then people began writing letters telling her the things she needed for the book, their letters arriving at timely intervals and just in time for her writing the next day.

"I was trying to remember my childhood and wanted to understand it," she said. A letter from a relative would arrive, and in it Kate would find an unsolicited explanation about a relative she had been writing about, and the letter told why the person had behaved in a certain way. This, Kate believed, was no accident or merely coincidence.

And bit by bit, she said, these experiences made it easier for her to forgive people in her life who had hurt her as a child. At the same time she was learning that she had tapped into some inner source of information and knowledge that was available to her at will.

She also began to acquire books that supplied her with critical explanations as they were needed to fill in her hefty manuscript that now covered a wide range of subjects.

One of the things she wanted to know was biblical definition of the Holy Spirit. She also wanted to know whether or not it had ever been considered a source of physical energy. God had been given so much credit for incredible acts of healing and power, she thought. The Bible had also said that He was within us. Was this how she had beaten cancer—by tapping into the Holy Spirit? She wondered and posed the question in her mind, then continued working on the book.

A short time later, she went to the public library in town. As she walked through the rows, a book fell off a shelf in front of her. The book was called *The Helper*, by Catherine Marshall. It was a book about the meaning of the Holy Spirit.

Although she would not find this out until years later, Tom Sawyer had a similar experience at a public library in upstate New York, where he lived near Rochester.

After his near-death experience, the name Max Planck kept popping into his head. Although he had only a high school education, Tom was compelled to seek out books about something he could describe then only vaguely as quantum. A librarian suggested he look in a section where they kept books on quantum mechanics and physics. Tom, like Kate, began to walk through the stacks; a book careened off a high shelf during this trip, landing in front of him. It was a book about Max Planck, the father of quantum physics.

Kate's scholarly search helped her sort out long-standing, ingrained religious beliefs she had once taken as the gospel truth. Now, however, she found herself able to analyze dogma and give it new perspective from a point of view she was clearly developing anew as she went along.

She had decided that whatever it was that had triggered her cure, it had all been a spiritual encounter. In an attempt to define what happened to her further, she turned to all of the so-called great books of religion. Barbara Harris, who did not know Kate then but would later meet her through Ken Ring, also chose this route early in her own conversion. Many others did too.

"A funny thing happened in most religions based on the Bible," Kate said one night while reading. It was clear to her that each one was making virtually the same claim about its interpretation of the Bible. "Everybody was saying their version was the absolute truth. But they kept giving God these escape routes." That night she decided God wasn't any of the things organized religion was claiming. She had met God and was developing her own definition, a process that began evolving in her head. He wasn't the entity the Catholic Church had used to scare the hell out of her.

That was when she began calling herself a "freelance person of God." Speaking to friends and her own priest once, she announced that "the Bible was pure truth, but people got their hands on it and did a little editing." Kate was prompted to become this self-defined, freelance worshiper, because it was becoming increasingly clear that the priests and elders of organized churches had been freelance interpreters of the Bible who concocted all sorts of ungodly claims in the name of their churches in God's name.

Realizing these things as she read clearly helped to trigger a turning point for what would be a continuing journey for Kate Valentine.

Somewhere along the way, she heard the name Ken Ring and contacted him in Connecticut. "I read one of his books and wrote him. I wanted to know more and he brought me to UConn," she said. After this initial contact, Kate and Paul moved back to Connecticut, this time settling in a house not far from Ring, near the university and just a few miles from the medical center.

Suddenly, Kate found herself lecturing on a private experience that people everywhere seemed to find captivating. "I started giving talks and doing whatever Ken wanted," said Kate, who appeared on numerous television and radio talk shows, including *Good Morning America, Larry King Live, and Sonia Live*. Barbara Harris, Tom Sawyer, Kathy Latrelle and Steve Price, in turn, were telling the world their stories too.

Briefly, Kate joined Bruce Greyson's support group, where she met Barbara, Steve, Kathy and dozens of others who also had transformation stories to tell. The group noted how their lives had shifted after their NDEs, and Kate knew this from her own experience.

Among the many aftereffects she knew had stemmed from her NDE was the way she disturbed electrical appliances. Kate not only had tapped into some unnamed vein of creative expression, she says she had also tapped into some sort of electromagnetic reservoir that affected things around her.

On a trip to Florida after her NDE, and before all of this activity gradually changed their lives, Kate and Paul finally had a conversation about the night she died.

The couple was walking down a quaint strip of shopping boutiques as the night sky settled in and the streetlights came on. While they strolled hand in hand, Kate felt the urge to finally tell Paul everything.

"Thank God," Paul said when she had finished. "I thought you were having an affair." He hugged Kate there on the street. "You seemed so relaxed, so peaceful, I was sure you had found a lover."

As he talked, they both noticed that something strange had occurred on the street. The lights in the storefronts were still on, but the streetlights had all gone out when Kate walked under each one.

"I have a profound effect on electrical appliances. Sometimes tape recorders don't record around me, and I fog up the film in people's cameras," she said. "I have the physical ability to vibrate things. We all vibrate at certain frequencies. I vibrate at a very high frequency and this opens up various channels of information for me," she told Paul that night. "I can reset other people's vibration rates as soon as they walk in my vicinity."

Joking, she said that most people are capable of tuning into these channels too, but "most of you guys are between channels," she said, kidding this man she talks about with all the adoration of a teenager in love for the first time.

Unable to technically identify what happens, Kate, Barbara Harris and others who have had similar experiences all tell similar stories. Barbara Harris once disabled every camera in a Michigan television studio where she and Bruce Greyson were supposed to tape a program about their work.

In a matter-of-fact way, Kate explains it as "some sort of magnetic thing" that affects everyone. This, she says, is one of the reasons people are being afflicted with new, modern illnesses.

"We are surrounded by microwaves, remote controls and other devices all operating on transmitted energy signals," she said. "People operate in similar ways using vibrational systems that malfunction because we are surrounded by electrical pollution from all these varied signals disrupting our own energy fields."

But for centuries man has known about a subtle biological force that in Sanskrit is called Kundalini. The word literally means to be coiled like a snake about to strike. Many ancients and modern-day discovers of Kundalini believe it is a dormant force that lies stored at the base of the spine. When activated, this energy shoots through channels in the body known as chakras. As it moves, it transforms the host's physical and psychological framework. Those who have studied the aftermath of this phenomenon call the event a Kundalini awakening and believe it hurls people who experience it into higher states of consciousness not unlike those described by Kate, Barbara Harris and others who have had NDEs.

These awakenings have also been reported by practitioners of yoga and meditation, and many say the transformations that follow are identical to those reported by NDE survivors.

These things and more were all revealed to Kate over a period of years. Her children, young at the time all this began happening, have grown up believing that blinking streetlights, malfunctioning electrical appliances and their mother's clairvoyant musings were natural. And some of these abilities were passed to others in the family.

"My daughter started doing it. We'd be talking about something passionate, and suddenly all the lights would go out," Kate said, laughing as she spoke. "My husband started to do it too, because they were living in spaces with me. We had one of those lamps that gets brighter and brighter every time you touch it. One day he walked into our bedroom alone and the lamp kept going on and off and it really ticked him off," she said. The family did not understand how or why this ability was transferred. But they all agreed it was sometimes disruptive.

Then others things began to happen.

"People kept coming to me asking for advice," said Kate, explaining why she had wanted to remain anonymous after an initial interview for this book.

"I don't need the notoriety," she continued, clearly wanting to avoid a repeat of something that happened to her over and over. "Cleaning ladies hired to do day work came, spent the day telling me their problems." Most did not know about her experience or how it had changed her. "Whenever my daughter or son came home from school and saw their mother sitting down, listening to the cleaning lady or the plumber, they'd take out the vacuum cleaner and start dusting the living room. They knew the house wasn't going to be cleaned that day, or the pipes weren't going to be fixed. Mom was fixing somebody," Kate joked.

"My children grew up with this kind of stuff happening all the time, so it was normal for them to see strangers sitting in our living room. Strange cars would just stall outside our house. They'd come in to use the phone and they'd start telling me their problems. When we finished talking, their cars always started and we'd never see them again," she said.

"I have this ability to know what's happening to people around me. I can feel their anger and I can tell why they're angry," she said, citing another problem her auspicious transformation created for her. This too was disruptive.

"One time a woman at a gym walked past me and I knew she had just fallen in love." Kate smiled, scanning the ceiling with her eyes as she spoke. "Remember the first time you fell in love in high school? It was that same kind of feeling. And I didn't just know it, I felt it. Later, I was listening to this woman talk to her girlfriends in the locker room as she was drying her hair, telling them about this guy, and I already knew the story," said Kate.

Another time, she and her daughter planned to go to a crafts fair not far from the UConn Medical Center, where she usually met Barbara Harris and the others for the monthly IANDS meetings. Although they didn't arrive until the fair was almost over, she went hoping to buy antiques she could strip, refinish and paint in her studio. They arrived about three in the afternoon. When she got there, Kate was cornered by a man who wanted to talk about his brother, who was dying of cancer.

"Now, you track this statistically," she said, laughing. "What are the odds that this man and I would be on those grounds at the same time?" she asked rhetorically. "He was a doctor who wanted me to reassure him that his brother would be okay. When I tell people my story, it gives them hope. Without hope, there is no life."

This kind of thing happened to Kate all the time. But these encounters weren't always so benign, and she paid an emotional price for knowing and seeing into the souls of the not-so-perfect strangers she happened across. And sometimes this ability literally scared the hell out of her.

One day while she and Paul were riding up quaint Main Street, their car pulled up alongside another vehicle stopped for the light. When Kate glanced over and made eye contact with the driver, she saw something that sickened and horrified her.

"I knew he was a pedophile. I knew he had just killed a child in some woods, and I knew he was from Canada. I couldn't block it out," she said, her eyes transfixed on some unseen, distant object as she spoke.

As others would later report, Kate did not just see things, she felt the emotions of the people involved. If the incident involved love, Kate felt in love. If the people she came in contact with were sad, depressed or angry, Kate experienced their sadness, depression or anger. It was almost as if she had multiple-personality disorder, a clinical term that fails to adequately explain this experience.

"Kate, you're like a 220-watt outlet for people. They plug into you and drain you," said Barbara Harris, who met Kate while Barbara worked in the IANDS office at the university medical center. Gradually, Barbara and others helped Kate learn ways to block these emotional signals. It's an acquired talent, though, she says, one that not everyone would be comfortable having.

"Anyone can tap into what we tapped into," she insists, as others also have. "We are just harbingers of the future. We're the people who went out there for whatever reason, were in the right place at the right time, and it just happened." She is echoing a claim made repeatedly by NDErs.

The message in her voice is a modest one:

These are human, not supernatural, events we are witnessing. We are just hearing about them on a scale that is unprecedented in our time.

"We are just a taste of what all human beings can and should be," says Kate.

CHAPTER TEN

∞

Mellen-Thomas Benedict

The story Anang told the shamans the day Mellen arrived in their jungle village in the Philippines had its unlikely beginnings on an American military base.

Growing up, Mellen had been shuttled from one base to another. He spent his first five years in Germany. After his mother divorced his GI father, she moved the family stateside. In 1960, when Mellen was eleven and his brother, Michael, was ten, she married another military man. Mellen's stepfather, Phil, was transferred to Tokyo a short time later and took the family with him.

Mellen loved Tokyo. He could ride the subways and wander streets, browse the shops and stalls, buy firecrackers on the cheap and gorge himself on tempura, a weakness. Nearly everyone spoke at least some English. Japan had yet to prove itself a postwar economic power, and Tokyo was a bargain for anyone with American dollars to spend.

More than the street life and the food, Mellen loved the Japanese ceremonies. There always seemed to be a ceremony around the corner, like the joyous summer celebration of the Star Festival, when marchers carried long streamers of bright paper and fabric through the streets. And there was the mysterious Day of the Dead, when families launched armadas of tiny boats bearing candles and messages for their ancestors.

The family lived in Tokyo for three years, until Mellen began his sophomore year in high school. Then they moved back to the States.

Phil moved them to a small Amish farm town outside a base in eastern Pennsylvania, and then, a year later, to Fayetteville, North Carolina. At the city high school, Mellen's teachers encouraged him to become an artist. He could draw exceptionally well and had an eye for photography. His senior year in Fayetteville, one teacher wrangled the 16 mm movie camera that the football team used to film Saturday games, and told Mellen to see what he could do with it. He produced a film, *The Enemy*, the story of a man chased by an unknown pursuer. Ultimately, the man realizes he is running from no one but himself. It was a heavy-handed first attempt. But the experience gave Mellen direction. It convinced him he wanted to be a famous filmmaker.

It was his still photography that helped get him his first job. An advertising agency in Atlanta saw a few stills that had won Mellen prizes in a national photography competition, and it asked him down for an interview. At the time, Mellen planned a much longer trip to Vietnam. Before he became a famous filmmaker, he intended to pack in a few years as a much-decorated helicopter pilot. Like most of the military brats connected to Fort Bragg, he wanted to fight the Communist threat to the free world. It was 1967, and more than 35,000 antiwar demonstrators had marched on the Pentagon. Protesters were occupying administrative buildings on college campuses to protest the expansion of the draft. Demonstrators had even disrupted Congress, dumping a torrent of antiwar leaflets on the Senate floor. But Fort Bragg was still well insulated from the jolts of the peace movement. Anxious to fight another good war himself, Phil had joined the Green Berets, the elite Army unit.

But then the letters started coming home. Long, despondent, sometimes desperate letters from Phil. He questioned the war and his role in it. It was hard to tell whose side the South Vietnamese were on, or to trust them, he complained. Not that he could blame them. Phil was no longer sure he was fighting for anyone's freedom or that life under Communism would be that much worse than it had been under colonialism. He didn't know what to believe. The war changed and embittered him.

"Don't go. It's a complete waste," Phil wrote his stepson. The advice came as something of a shock to Mellen. If his own father, a Green Beret, said the war was a mistake, then maybe the official line on Vietnam was suspect. Mellen had already been down to the recruiting office to enlist. But he ran into a problem during the physical. It was his knee, still badly scarred from a fall in the fifth grade. He was classified 4-F, medically unfit for combat, but he planned to fight the classification. After hearing from Phil, he let it go. The ad agency in Atlanta offered him a job and he took it.

By 1968, a good century after General Sherman had burned Atlanta to its foundation, the city was thriving. With a population of 500,000, it was ten times the size of Fayetteville and had much more to offer. There were more than thirty colleges and universities, museums, bookstores and clubs. The job at the ad agency was a good one. It was a small place where everyone did everything—plotted campaign strategy, worked on storyboards, designed sets, edited tape. Mellen got close to a number of the art directors and copywriters and met other friends through them. They'd get together at one another's homes and talk.

His girlfriend, Linda, introduced him to metaphysics. Every now and then, she'd take him to bookstores with good collections. Mellen read a bit about Taoism for a while. But his interest in spirituality was intermittent and peripheral. After a year at the ad agency, he set up as a freelancer, hiring himself out for both TV commercials and feature films. His work was central.

And he enjoyed it. Work was often exciting, rarely ordinary. Some days bordered on the absurd, like the one he spent slicing through candy bar after candy bar with a razor. They were shooting a commercial and needed a bar that really looked like it was "packed with peanuts." He' went through dozens before he found one that fit the bill.

Through his contacts in TV, Mellen started getting tips about feature films that were under production. He'd sign on to work the camera, or handle the sound equipment, or stage the stunts, or take over as second director. The vast majority of the films were action flicks with speeding cars in the lead roles. They were shot in dusty little towns in south Georgia and central Arizona. The big thing was to come up with some new twist in the plot, some new combination of chase-and-crash scenes. The crew's best effort was a scene in which a car crashed through a tractor-trailer truck, driving the truck through a house. The finishing touch—a shot of a half-dozen people bailing out the windows and door as the house exploded— looked like it would be hard to cast. But the crew finally tracked down a chapter of Hell's Angels, whose members were happy to oblige as stuntmen.

Work was also an escape from the ennui that began to gnaw at Mellen. These were disillusioning times. Martin Luther King Jr. had been assassinated in Memphis and racially segregated inner-city neighborhoods like Watts and Roxbury were burning. Civil rights workers were being beaten and killed in the South. Presidential-hopeful Robert Kennedy was gunned down. Demographers warned of a population explosion.

The bill for the rapid industrial expansion and suburban sprawl of the 1950s was coming due. Smog gathered over Los Angeles; environmentalists declared Lake Erie officially dead due to dumping. The arms race continued apace. Nuclear weapons' stockpiles kept mounting, as did the body count in the Vietnam War. The nation gathered around TV sets in 1974 to watch Richard Nixon, his presidency shadowed by the Watergate scandal, duck into a helicopter and leave Washington after resigning in disgrace.

It was a frightening time. Institutions were unreliable, people untrustworthy. That was how Mellen came to view it all. Things looked bleak. After a while, even the crazy camaraderie and absurd excess of the car-crash movie sets began to lose their appeal. The money was good. And he still wanted to do feature films, but different ones. Something else.

Walking around downtown Atlanta one afternoon, he happened upon a stained-glass show at a local gallery. He was impressed. He never realized how versatile and expressive glass could be. After a few classes, he had the basics down. Before long, he was studying with local artists whose work he admired. Not long after that, he opened his own stained-glass studio, East of Eden Stained Glass.

In 1978, he moved the studio from Atlanta to Fayetteville, North Carolina, where his mother and stepfather lived. And that was when the blackouts began. The first time he blacked out, he was sitting at home alone. He came to quickly, and since he was healthy otherwise, he decided it was nothing to worry about.

But the blackout was followed by another, and then by many others. Shortly before he'd lose consciousness, he'd feel weak and dizzy; then everything would go black. That was a warning sign. Driving in the car with his girlfriend one afternoon, he sensed trouble. He asked her to get behind the wheel, and then he blacked out. When he came to, the car was pulled to the side of the road. His girlfriend was cradling his face in her hands. She insisted he see a doctor.

Mellen found a general practitioner who sent him to a specialist for tests. There were blood tests and bone scans and finally a CT scan that showed quite clearly what the problem was. It was a brain tumor. There was worse news to come. The tumor was malignant and it was inoperable. The location precluded surgery, and though chemotherapy would slow it's growth, that would not stop it. And there would be side effects.

"The chemo won't stop it, but it may slow it down and give you more time," the oncologist said. "Unfortunately, it won't be quality time." Mellen asked what that meant.

"You'll become a sort of vegetable," the doctor explained. "To be honest with you, and I think I should be, you'll have to have someone change your diapers at the end."

Mellen was sure the oncologist was wrong, so he found a second specialist. But the prognosis was unchanged. Six to eight months. He couldn't accept that. How could he have only six to eight months to live? What kind of life was this anyway?

His disillusionment turned to disgust. What was the purpose of it all? All people managed to do was screw things up, kill one another, poison the planet, overrun it. What were they here for anyway?

For a few weeks he followed his usual routine. He drove to the studio, opened it, assembled his tools. But he couldn't concentrate. He'd sit in silence, the sun filtering green and ruby and royal blue through the stained glass he'd hung in his windows. Eventually, he accepted the prognosis. He was going to die. There were certain eventualities to plan for. He wouldn't be able to work much longer, or drive himself around. The blackouts were already so frequent, it was surprising he hadn't been in a car accident already.

He decided not to tell his parents. His mother would insist on pursuing treatment, some kind of treatment, any kind. He knew she'd go as far as mortgaging the house to pay for it. There was no point in that. Instead, he confided in a handful of friends. Anxious to do what they could, they offered to help with transportation and chores.

As it turned out, the one who helped the most was Susan, a friend of a friend. Several weeks had passed since the diagnosis and Mellen had started having bouts with pain. It could be excruciating. All-consuming. Conventional pain killers had little effect. Morphine was a help, but the drug left him feeling so exhausted, he reluctantly gave it up. Coming home from a shopping trip with Susan one day, he had an episode of intense pain. Every fiber of his body was in agony. He groaned. He felt Susan's hand on his neck, and suddenly the pain vanished.

"What did you do?" he asked, dumbfounded. There was no pain at all. Susan said she wasn't sure what she'd done. She seemed to have this peculiar ability. She'd used it with her children when they were ill, and with the terminal patients she'd helped when she was a hospice volunteer.

They got together a week or so later and drove to Wilmington, North Carolina, for a walk along the beach. They talked. Susan told Mellen about hospice. It provided care and comfort to the terminally ill, she said. The aim of hospice was to keep the patient comfortable, free of pain. That was more or less when they decided that Susan would be Mellen's hospice volunteer. Her children were grown up and out of the house. She was single again, rather well off and looking for something to do. What an amazing, amazing woman this is, he thought.

For a while, Susan cared for Mellen at his house. Ultimately, they decided he should move somewhere outside Fayetteville where they wouldn't have to worry about his parents' reaction to his unexplained decline. Another friend agreed to lend her vacation cottage in the mountains. So, in the oppressive heat of a North Carolina summer, they moved. Mellen told his parents that he wanted a change of scenery and would probably be out of touch for a while. At that point he had just months to live. The plan was to have Susan explain everything to his parents after his death.

A couple hours' drive from Fayetteville, the cottage was ideal. It was clean and cozy, with wonderful views of the mountains all around. Oddly enough, it had a good collection of books about metaphysics. *The Tibetan Book of the Dead* was there and Mellen started reading. It was heavy going. He couldn't understand much. But it piqued his interest. The next time he and Susan went out, he asked her to stop at the public library, where he found a book about world religions. He finished that and wanted to know more. The next trip downtown, he borrowed several more books from the library. He began to read everything he could find about death and the afterlife.

He read about the Hindu doctrine of reincarnation, which dictated that each soul should live through successive deaths and rebirths. Those who lived righteously could expect to be reborn under more auspicious circumstances. Those born to suffering and poverty were paying the wages of sins committed in previous lives. According to one Hindu legend, a woman who burned with jealousy in one life was reborn as a chili pepper in the next. Only after innumerable lives of righteousness might a soul escape the cycle of rebirth and achieve ecstatic union with Brahman, the god above all gods.

Buddhist theology promised a faster way out of the cycle of death and rebirth. The way to break the cycle was to achieve serenity by letting go of desire—desire for power, wealth, fame, success and all other worldly things. The Buddha, who achieved this state of enlightenment in meditation, was said to have announced at his birth, "This is my last existence."

Then there was Judaism, far more ambiguous about the hereafter. "Know that just as a blind man can form no idea of colors nor a deaf man comprehend sounds, so bodies cannot comprehend the delights of the soul," Maimonides had written. Among Jews, there seemed to be a wide range of interpretation, from belief in resurrection to a conviction that death truly was the end.

Islam promised a last day of judgment. On this day everyone would receive a record of his deeds in life. The book would be placed in the right hand of the good, who would go to heaven, and in the left hand of the evil, who would go to hell. While hell would be a place of agony and torture, heaven would be a place of exuberant joy, crowded with beautiful dark-eyed maidens.

Mellen realized his own vague notions of the afterlife were still rooted in his childhood understanding of Christian doctrine. God was up in heaven above, and down below was the Devil in hell. After death, the virtuous were rewarded in heaven and the sinners were punished in hell. He was no longer certain what happened at death, But he believed that something essential—call it the soul—lived on in some way.

"For the first time, I began thinking about those things," he told Ken Ring when they met years later. "I started boning up. My idea was, I didn't want to be surprised. I thought I was behind on religion and had better check it out. Then, whoever I met, I could at least tell them I've read your book."

Though the original prognosis gave Mellen only a few months to live, he and Susan spent six months at the cottage. By the end of that time, he had talked her into doing something she had objected to strenuously at first. After all his reading, he was convinced his body should be left undisturbed immediately after death, the better to allow his spirit to disengage from the physical world. He got Susan to agree to leave it undisturbed for at least a couple of hours.

One spring morning, when the leaves were out but the dawn was still accompanied by reminders of winter's cold, Mellen awoke early and knew this was the day. The bedside alarm clock said 4:30. The blackouts had become so frequent by now that he was unconscious for long stretches. He'd wake up disoriented and had fallen into the habit of checking the clock as soon as he awoke. As the blackouts had grown more frequent and longer, he'd grown progressively weaker.

Certain this was the day, he called for Susan. She came into the room. They talked. He thanked her for all she had done. They held each other for a while. And then she left to let him make some phone calls. He called two friends to tell them good-bye. In retrospect, he wasn't sure he was thinking clearly. Both friends had known he was dying. They began to cry. His friend Bill, whom he called in New York, reminded Mellen about a drawing. Mellen had given him the drawing years earlier. Bill said he would always remember him by it.

"Why don't you get a frame for it, then? You've had it all this time," Mellen joked. They said good-bye. That conversation over, he lay back and drifted into what felt like an infinitely deep sleep.

CHAPTER ELEVEN

∽

Steve Price

Whatever it was that had kept Steve from firing his M-16 during his second Vietnam tour of duty in 1968, it began to change him.

Although that change began during his first combat tour when a mortar fragment nearly killed him, it would take him more than twenty years to realize what had really happened to him.

But Steve's story begins with that first tour in Vietnam in 1965.

His unit was part of Operation Harvest Moon, an annual campaign launched in September to keep valuable rice crops from falling into enemy hands. Dressed in a flak jacket, vehicle mechanic Steve Price had been in-country for less than a month when Charley Company moved out on this tactical mission. Steve rode in a vehicle as the company headed out about three miles from Da Nang, within sight of Marble Mountain.

A short time after they started, the order to dig in came and they halted to make camp. The unit set up night defenses as it rapidly began to grow dark. Conveniently, many of these combat-weary soldiers found mortar pits from an enemy shelling sometime earlier.

"Our people dug them out a little and we were settled in less than fifteen minutes," Steve said.

The unit had walked into an ambush but didn't know it. Now the enemy could zero in on the Marines' position with deadly accuracy by simply firing mortars using old coordinates. The moon was hidden behind clouds, despite the name of this mission, when the attack came.

The VC had precisely measured off the distance from those pits to their mortars. After Steve's unit had settled in, the enemy just clobbered the soldiers by lobbing mortar shells right on top of them. Unable to see even their closest buddies in the dark, the Marines snuggled in for the night; then all hell broke loose.

To make an already chaotic situation worse, the Americans thought they were hearing their own mortar fire, return rounds they thought were falling short of VC targets and bursting over their own heads. The rounds weren't short, and the unit began taking heavy casualties from VC mortars.

Fortunately, Steve hadn't dug in yet. He was still riding on top of a vehicle when the shooting started.

"I knew we weren't hearing short rounds. I decided to jump down and crawl under the vehicle I was on." Just as he started to jump, he said, mortars exploded about thirty feet above his head, showering him with white-hot shrapnel.

Holding his rifle high in the air with one hand, Steve was about to jump for cover when he noticed something molten hurtling his way.

"I saw a serrated coil coming right for me," he said. Two slivers of the metal sliced through his shirt under one armpit and cut into his chest just above the flak jacket.

"I am hit," he yelled as he fell from the truck.

"Bullshit," someone yelled back at him. "Get your ass back up here."

The last thing Steve remembered was calling for the Navy medics who always traveled with the unit. But his mind began to race in multiple directions at once.

First he remembered his boot-camp training. Gaping, sucking chest wound.

What to do?

"Always cover a chest wound. Keeps the lungs from collapsing."

Check!

Steve clamped his arm down, pulling it as tightly against his chest as he could. The corpsman crawled up next to him, rolled him over and started to dress the wound.

The medic shot him up, pumping a heavy dose of morphine into his shivering body. It dulled the pain.

But Steve's body began to throb and he was shivering even worse; in this stinking jungle heat, he was freezing. That meant only one thing. Shit! Shock—he was going into shock.

Every soldier knew that shock was the biggest killer in battle. Fight it off. Stay alert. Keep your head, stay alert, you stay alive, he remembered from boot camp. He recited his military-service number over and over again. Remembered his home address in Connecticut and said it over and over again.

But Steve began to lose, slipping farther and farther away into some other realm of consciousness.

It might have been the effects of the drugs the

corpsman had shot into him, or what would later be identified as a surge of a natural bio energy that some mystics call Kundalini. Whatever it was, it surged through Steve and he had an out-of-body experience; then he went through the classic stages of the NDE.

"I saw myself as a baby. I saw the things my father did to me and I saw a lot of things I really didn't want to remember," he said, almost teary-eyed as he spoke. "I saw everything that happened in my life."

One of the things he didn't want to see was the sight of himself stealing money from his ailing grandfather.

"I saw it all over again," he said. "My grand-father was old, eight-nine years old when he died, and he spent the last five years of his life bedridden. Even though he hadn't left that bed in five years, he kept his trousers at the foot of the bed and always had money in his pants.

"I saw myself stealing twenty bucks from him in that life review. I was about eight years old, and in the review I was judging myself, saying, 'Steve, what are you doing?' I was lying wounded in Vietnam, feeling pretty bad about something I had done to my grandfather, and at that point I hated myself," he said.

"I knew I wasn't dead, but I kept seeing these pictures of my life in my mind and thought I was about to die. I felt relieved when the life review ended, totally relieved, the way a child is relieved when they get a spanking and it suddenly ends," said Steve.

Meanwhile, choppers were called in and Steve and the other wounded were evacuated to a nearby medical field unit. Steve later awoke, groggy, in a medical tent and regained consciousness just long enough to overhear someone say, "If he makes it through the night, he might make it."

The next time he awoke, he was being loaded onto a C-141 medical air transport plane bound for Clark Air Base in the Philippines. When the plane touched down at Clark, ten patients were loaded aboard school buses for the short ride to the base hospital. Steve, however, was hustled into an awaiting ambulance.

Two days later, doctors operated to inflate his collapsed lung. That was when it happened again.

After receiving a pre-op injection that nearly put him to sleep, a still groggy but partially conscious Steve was wheeled out into a hallway. The gurney he lay on was parked right next to a red brick wall. What happened next might have been induced simply by the drugs and pain killers the nurses had given him. He might have experienced hallucinations or the vivid dreams sometimes associated with anesthesia. Steve would later be convinced it was a continuing part of an NDE and the start of a multi-year trek toward understanding things more profound than anything he might conjure up in a mere dream.

"I remember thinking how strange that wall looked," he said. As ill as he had apparently been before his operation, Steve said he suddenly felt well. "My pain was gone and I could breathe easily." Then something even more surprising happened.

"I left my body and I was up on the ceiling looking down at myself, and I remember saying, 'Hey, dummy, what are you doing down there? It's time to go—let's go.' "

At that point, Steve said, he turned around to face the brick wall and the wall became light.

"That light was God, and He didn't give a damn that I had done all of this stuff, and was just going to hold me for a while. I don't ever remember being held in such a loving way," said Steve.

Then the scene shifted again.

"I left the light and was in this place where there was a stream. On the other side of the stream I saw my grandfather standing there in his nightshirt, just as I remembered him from 1953, when he died," said Steve.

"Behind him, I saw a wild yet orderly forest and everything was perfect. There were trees and flowers, and the colors aren't in our color scheme." Everything glowed, he said, "as if they were neon, and I think that was because everything was filled with God's light. My grandfather suddenly told me it wasn't my time.

" 'You've got to go back,' he told me.

" 'I don't want to go back,' I said, knowing that all I had to do in order to stay was jump over the stream in front of me to the other side." Steve tried to jump.

Instantly, he was hurled backward into his body and found himself awake, lying in a hospital bed. The operation was over. He was back in his room.

Upon waking, he said, he was so sorrowful about his abrupt return that he began to sob. He cried, he said, because he was certain he was being punished. He kept seeing glimpses of himself stealing money from his grandfather, and kept hearing himself being ordered out of this heavenly place.

Confused and dazed, he blurted all of this out to the nurse on duty at the time.

"You're on a lot of drugs," she told him. "You're having hallucinations."

Steve believed her then and shut up.

But he had noticed something significant that told him that she was wrong.

Whenever I get a shot of morphine, it dulls the pain, but I always know it's there, he thought. Also, he could move freely in and out of this peaceful light that had enveloped him earlier. And whenever he went to the light, the pain disappeared completely.

"When I was in the light, the pain was completely gone," Steve said. There was something about the light that could not be explained away, even though it was easy to blame the phenomenon on the drugs he was taking. Some weeks later, he was flown to St. Albans, a military hospital in New York, to convalesce. He continued to see the light and it began to haunt him.

As he recovered and gained his strength, Steve said he took up drinking heavily.

"I was trying to block out the light," he explained. "Part of me believed I had been punished, and seeing the light just reminded me of it, so I drank. Sometimes I drank just so I could sleep."

Fully fit and recovered by 1968, Steve Price could easily have sat out the remaining years of the war. Instead, he volunteered for a second tour. Promoted to staff sergeant, he could now command grunts in the field who would respect his experience. Every sailor, soldier and airman in the United States military could wear a Vietnam era medal whether he had served in-country or not. That medal just meant you had joined up in that era. But Steve also wore the Purple Heart. On a second tour, he could wind up with a cluster surrounding that medal if he got hit again and lived. So he re-upped for a second tour and was shipped out again.

But when he arrived in-country this time, something unimaginable came over him. As he was being issued an M-16 automatic weapon, something decisive clearly told him that he could not kill.

"I did everything I was supposed to do, but I never fired that weapon, even though I was in heavy combat," this career soldier said. "I was a Marine and Marines are trained to shoot people. I was a staff sergeant, so I told people to keep their heads down. I taught people how to use their weapons, but I just couldn't fire my own." He lived out the remainder of his tour without incident. Instead of a weapon, the thing that Steve carried and which he most identified with was the light, not his weapon.

In 1969, he was rotated back to the States, where he had planned to continue his life as a career soldier.

But that wasn't to be either.

CHAPTER TWELVE

∽

Kathy Latrelle

It was routine surgery, Kathy Latrelle's doctor told her. It was nothing to worry about, particularly at her age. She was what, twenty-four? he asked, looking at her chart.

There was absolutely nothing to worry about. She should come in January 23. The surgery would take only a few hours, and she'd be out the same day; no big deal.

How would he know? Kathy thought, watching him flip through his appointment book. He was a man talking about vaginal surgery. He'd never had it. Besides, it was 1979, and January 23 was going to be her twenty-fifth birthday. A day in the hospital wasn't her idea of a celebration. Alan was still in Turkey; he'd been there a year now. But her mother and Ted were planning a birthday celebration for her.

"The twenty-third is my birthday," Kathy said.

"Sorry, you need to take care of this right away," the doctor told her. Kathy had gone to this doctor, a specialist, after she started bleeding between her periods. It was uncomfortable, but she didn't think

119

it was an emergency. He insisted, though, and she reluctantly agreed to come in on the twenty-third.

Her mother picked her up for the drive to Hartford Hospital that morning. Kathy had been back in Connecticut for several months now. She'd found a job in a doctor's office. She, her mother and Ted were getting along better.

At the hospital, a nurse showed Kathy to an examining room near the operating suite. Though the operation would be brief, it could be painful, and that was why they planned to use general anesthesia, the nurse told her. Lying on the gurney while they wheeled her down the hall and into the suite, Kathy wished it were over.

In the suite, Kathy had a view of the ceiling, a view that was interrupted now and then by the green-masked chins, noses and eyeglasses of the surgeon, the nurses and the anesthesiologist as they bent over her. She was studying one of the acoustic tiles when she felt herself slipping away. She closed her eyes.

When she opened them again, something peculiar had happened. Her perspective had changed. She wasn't looking up at the ceiling and the surgeon anymore, but at someone on a gurney just like hers in the same room, off to her side. More peculiar still, she couldn't get her eyes open. Nonetheless, Kathy could see this person, a woman with long blond hair, lying on the gurney. She knew it was no dream. It was as real as her drive to the hospital just an hour earlier. And she knew the woman on the gurney was in trouble,

The woman had begun to vomit, and because she was sedated, she began to choke and suffocate. A surgeon and nurses in green surgical pajamas were standing around her, but they hadn't realized yet what was happening. Kathy knew the problem was with the anesthesia. But the anesthesiologist wasn't anywhere in the room.

Kathy began to panic. She wanted to get the doctor's attention, tell him the woman next to her needed help. She tried to shout the words "Help her!" but couldn't make a sound. Then she felt a sensation she had never felt before. It was as though her entire body, from her head to her feet, was stretching, getting longer. There was a tingling tension all over her body. And before she had a chance to sort out exactly what was happening, she found herself floating up in a corner of the operating room.

Rising eight feet off the floor, she could see, in detail, everything below. She wasn't wearing her contact lenses—she'd had to remove them in pre-op—but everything was absolutely clear. Another peculiarity. She could see the doctor and nurses huddled over the gurney and the woman lying there. For the first time, she recognized the woman. It was she herself. Kathy wasn't the least bit upset any longer, though. It didn't even seem strange to be floating up near the ceiling.

This is me up here; down there is my body, she thought. But she wasn't really thinking either. The thought was there, but it hadn't come in words; it was expressed without words. None of that seemed disturbing. Kathy felt absolutely calm. She was watching with detachment, simply out of curiosity. It's my body, but so what? That's where I usually live, but now I'm up here.

Down below, the surgeon had finally realized the woman on the gurney was in trouble, and he started screaming for the anesthesiologist. Kathy watched the anesthesiologist run back into the room and begin suctioning her.

The anesthesiologist, surgeon and nurses were in a panic, frantically checking her vital signs. After watching for a few moments, however, Kathy grew bored with the scene and started looking around. She wanted to figure out where she was. Off to her right, she could see ceiling lights.

When she looked down again, though, it was as if she were viewing the scene below through a fish-eye lens. The operating room had become very tiny. It seemed very, very far away. Though Kathy was still in the corner, she realized she was also in the midst of a wondrous, otherworldly light.

Her body was down there dying; she knew this now. But she wasn't worried there in the light. For the first time in her life, she wasn't worrying about anything. She wasn't worrying about what anyone was thinking of her, not her parents or her teachers or the other kids at school, nor her commanding officer or Alan. She wasn't worrying anymore about what she was going to do with her life. In the light, she felt utterly serene, accepted, loved completely. And she loved. Without judging, she felt love for her parents, for Alan, for everyone who came to mind.

The light, she knew, was love. And it was limitless. She was part of it, but, somehow still separate. It was as if she were her own kind of light, not as bright as the light she was in. The light itself was dazzling, brighter than anything she'd ever seen, and yet it didn't hurt her to look at it. Looking at it was joyous.

She knew there were others in the light as well. They were a different quality of light behind the light. They weren't material, just shapes. They were so welcoming. She knew the shapes were the spirits of relatives who had died. She knew her great-grandparents and grandparents were there. And she knew her father was going to be there soon. That was when she realized he didn't have long to live.

Kathy couldn't have identified any of the relatives who were there, though she knew even her great-grandparents from old photographs. She couldn't have identified them by name. But she knew they were there with the others, that they were waiting for her and they loved her. She realized then that she had a choice: to stay or to return. And she realized it was all right with them if she decided to return.

But she couldn't make up her mind. She knew she had good reason to go back. She was young, had things to do. Yet there were reasons not to go back. Her life had been full of pain and difficulty and disappointment. She and Alan were separated. The people she worked with didn't like her, nor she them. But then again, she was only twenty-five. She had a long life ahead of her. Things could change.

I know I'm going to die, but do I really want to die today? she thought, considering the question with absolute calm. It's my twenty-fifth birthday. I'm not that old. I still have a life to live. Do I want to stay here?

She sensed a wall behind her, a barrier. And she knew intuitively that if she crossed this barrier, she would be choosing not to return. The barrier wasn't physical, and she no longer had a physical body. Still, she was afraid that, always clumsy, she'd stumble backward over the wall without meaning to. She could end up tripping into eternity. She tried not to move.

I need more time, she thought.

That was when the life review began. It was as though she'd suddenly stepped into an enormous movie screen on which scenes from her life were playing in three dimensions. She saw good things she had done and bad things, people she'd hurt and people she'd helped.

Suddenly she was back in the parking lot in front of Caldor's. It was night, the store was closing and she noticed a woman having trouble starting her car. The battery had died. Kathy watched herself give the woman a jump-start. And then she saw something that hadn't happened but would have, had she not intervened. Kathy watched a man appear and approach the woman, stranded in the parking lot with a car that wouldn't start. He threatened her and took her purse.

She saw other scenes from her life, not only as herself, but as others who had played roles; not only watching them, but feeling as they had felt.

Through the light, she saw herself back in her bed that night her father had sobbed and shouted on the phone. She was thirteen again, afraid to get out of bed or to sleep, sweating in her pajamas, the covers around her chin. And she was her father, so frightened, unable to control himself. And she was her mother, worried and despairing. She lived that night as all three of them. Their feelings were distinct, but she felt them all at once.

She relived another night. She was her mother on another night, standing by a sink full of dirty dishes, exhausted and crying. Kathy remembered that she'd refused to help with the dishes, but she never knew her mother had been so hurt.

She went through a third day, the day when one of her parents' friends had sexually assaulted her. She was nine at the time. She went through the ordeal again as herself and as her parents. They had been heartbroken, and she felt their anguish now. Kathy even went through that day as the man who had molested her. She felt as he had felt, angry and confused.

Kathy relived a few dozen other benchmarks in her life, periods of profound feeling that changed her life. The scenes played out phenomenally quickly. She relived all of them in a matter of about ten seconds, she realized later.

She knew, at the end of the review, that, given the circumstances of her life, she could have come up with plenty of excuses for becoming embittered, for turning away completely. But she'd chosen not to, over and over. She relived times when she hadn't helped people. But she relived many other occasions when she had. She understood that this was of the utmost importance.

She couldn't decide whether to go back. The light was bliss. Life was difficult.

If I step over this wall behind me, it'll be forever and it'll be nice and I can feel like this forever, but there'll be no motorcycles she thought, surprised that that particular thought had come to her, but suddenly reexperiencing the simple joy of careening down a forest path on her dirt bike.

So she was given a glimpse into her future.

She saw a serpentine path stretch out below her. Some sections of the path glowed in brilliant colors, every color of the spectrum. At its brightest, the path was a glowing yellow. In sections the yellow gave way to brilliant, glowing orange, then red, then violet and finally a deep blue and black. Kathy understood that the bright sections were times of joy in her life; the dark, times of loss and pain.

She saw that at the beginning of the path, and knew this was her life in her twenties, with the dark spots and light spots. Her thirties were a gradient of color, starting with a long swath of bright yellow, then turning blue and finally black. The path remained black for a while, before growing lighter again. She knew the dark section would be a time of terrible loss and death. It wouldn't be her mother whom she would lose. It would be someone else whom she didn't yet care for as she would then.

The path stretched on through her forties, fifties and sixties.

Finally Kathy saw the end of her life. She wasn't sure whether she would live through her early eighties, but knew that she would be debilitated at the end, most likely unable to think for herself. It seemed that she would suffer a stroke and spend her last few years in a wheelchair. She understood that there was pain along the way, all through her life, but that there was also great joy. She couldn't have one without the other.

Kathy was contemplating the part of her life that lay immediately ahead, bright yellow leading gradually to black, when she thought of her dog Toofer. She saw the dog, a crazy salad of Labrador retriever and German shepherd. Toofer was black with brown markings and tan legs, a white blaze on her chest and a curly tail, like a pig's tail. No matter how depressed Kathy might feel, Toofer could crack her up, cheer her up, by wagging that crazy tail. She adored that dog. They went everywhere together. She took Toofer with her to the store, to the motorcycle shop. Toofer was a one-person dog. No one else wanted her. Kathy saw that the dog would be put to sleep if she didn't come back.

I have to go back for Toofer, Kathy thought. And immediately, she was back.

She was back on the gurney; she was vomiting; she started crying.

"Oh, oh, I want to go back," she wailed. The surgeon looked at her peculiarly.

∽

CHAPTER THIRTEEN

Mellen-Thomas Benedict

When Mellen opened his eyes, he found himself hovering high above the floor in his room, looking down at his body in bed. He realized he was near death. And he was frightened.

But then he saw the light. It was brilliant, more brilliant than any light he had ever seen. It was warm and inviting. Still, he realized that if he went to the light, he would die. He wanted time. Without saying the words, he asked for time. Immediately, he stopped moving.

"Is the light God?" he asked.

Then the light began to change. It started to take the shape of a man, with arms and legs and a head. Mellen recognized the brilliant image taking shape before him. It was Jesus. The image looked just like the portraits of Jesus that Mellen remembered from his catechism at boarding school. A thin man in a simple, belted robe, with long hair, a beard, a mustache and eyes that expressed inexhaustible compassion and love.

As Mellen watched, the light transformed itself again, this time becoming the patriarch Abraham.

Again, the image was similar to those he remembered from boarding-school religious instruction, whose books showed portraits of Abraham prepared to sacrifice his son Isaac to prove his faith in God. Abraham was dressed in a long robe, his feet dusty from his journey from Mesopotamia to Canaan, his face careworn.

Next, the light showed itself as Brahman, the thousand-headed Hindu god of gods. The light shifted and flickered as Brahman took the form of all thirty-three million Hindu gods—all manifestations of Brahman. The light became the god Vishnu, the preserver, resembling a man but clearly set apart by the third eye in his forehead. This was the Hindu eye of higher consciousness. Vishnu next took the shapes of his ten chief avatars, the forms in which he was said to descend to earth. Vishnu became Krishna, who spent his life helping mankind.

Krishna was dressed as a charioteer, just as he was in illustrations from the Bhagavad-Gita, the epic poem in which he accompanies the hero Arjuna in battle. The light then became the Hindu god Siva, the destroyer and restorer of life, and lord of the dance of creation. As in manuscripts Mellen had seen, Siva's throat was blue from his drinking the cup of men's sins for their salvation. He was dancing the dance of creation, one foot on the prostrate form of a dwarf who represented human ignorance. In his right hand Siva was carrying a small drum symbolizing creation, and in his left hand he held the fire of destruction.

Mellen watched, rapt, as the light rearranged itself again and became Siddhartha Gautama, the historical Buddha. With a look of absolute serenity on his face, the Buddha sat cross-legged in meditation, his right hand touching the ground. Mellen had seen paintings and statues showing Buddha in this same position, seated in meditation under the fig tree where he had achieved enlightenment twenty-five hundred years earlier. The light next took the form of a multitude of bodhisattvas, Buddhist saints who had reached the threshold of enlightenment, but postponed their own passage to nirvana to help others find their way to salvation.

Then the light took the shape of Mohammed. The prophet's face was veiled in an aureole of flame, just as it had been in the miniatures that Mellen remembered from his reading. Many depicted the prophet kneeling in prayer beside the Kaaba, Mecca's ancient shrine. The Kaaba contained a volcanic rock said to have been borne to earth by the angel Gabriel. Other miniatures showed Mohammed praying before Gabriel, come to tell the prophet, "Thou art the Messenger of God."

The light continued to change. It became a snake goddess from Crete, her waist draped with serpents. It took the shape of an ancient fertility goddess with bulging breasts, belly and buttocks. Next it was an Egyptian god with a jackal's head and a man's body. It was an owl goddess, with a woman's body but with a beak, enormous heavy-lidded eyes and pointed, tufted ears. The light took forms Mellen couldn't recall having seen before. He understood that these were gods and prophets from religions that archaeologists and historians could only conjecture about.

It dawned on Mellen that the light was reflecting back to him his own beliefs and knowledge. Raised in the Catholic Church, he'd been taught that Jesus was the Son of God, the Messiah. The image of Jesus he remembered from his school days had been reflected back to him in the light. Likewise, the images of Abraham and Mohammed and Brahman and Siva that he had studied during the past few months had been reflected back.

"Who is the real God?" he asked. And the answer came to him, unspoken, through the light. It was: I am. As Mellen understood this, the answer was that God was all things. God was all people, all life, the planets, the solar system, the universe, the sum total of everything.

He was surprised. "Why is humanity part of God? We're so evil," Mellen said, expressing the thought without speaking.

He then saw an enormous wheel of brilliant light. He understood that he was looking into a mosaic of human souls. The wheel of light was all colors and inexpressibly beautiful. He was taken into the light, and found himself in the depths of human souls. He visited the souls of saints, murderers, mothers, fathers, children, the brilliant, the wounded. He was astonished to find that there was no evil in any soul.

"How can this be?" he asked. The answer was that no soul was inherently evil. The terrible things that happened to people might make them do evil things, but their souls weren't evil. What all people seek, what sustains them, is love, the light told him. What distorts people is a lack of love.

Mellen was next shown life in the jungle. He looked out on a jungle glade. In the hazy distance he could make out low hills, a pale blue watering hole and lush gold grassland. Here and there were enormous deep green shade trees.

Crouching in the grass was a lion. Its powerful shoulders were arched back as it watched some gazelles grazing near the watering hole. Zebras and wildebeests, grazed nearby. There was a slow and steady rattle of hooves on the dry ground.

Suddenly the lion broke free and began to run toward the gazelles. The ground trembled with the accelerating drumming of hooves as the animals fled. But there was one gazelle that was slower than the rest, and steadily the lion closed in on it. When the lion was almost within striking distance, the gazelle began to run in half circles and spirals, desperate to escape. Within minutes the lion had the panting animal down on the ground, its jaws around the gazelle's neck. Mellen watched it begin to devour the gazelle.

"Is that evil?" the light asked. Mellen knew it was not. The lion had to kill to survive. "Men still hunt and prey on one another like animals because they are still evolving," the light told him.

Mellen asked whether animals and other living things also lied, as men did.

So he was shown exotic plants with features that mimicked the sex organs of insects—the better to get the insects to attempt to mate with and pollinate them. He watched as a wasp approached an orchid, attracted by its scent. The flower's petals bore a striking resemblance to the wings of the female wasp. Attracted initially by the scent, the male wasp lit on the flower, mistaking it for a female, and attempted to mate. Pollen from the flower covered his head. And after, when the wasp attempted to mate with another orchid, he inadvertently cross-pollinated it. This, Mellen realized, was as much a lie as anything men were capable of.

Watching, he felt as if he were observing a movie but was part of it. The next scenes were familiar. They were from his own life. He saw himself as a child at boarding school, in Tokyo and in Pennsylvania. He saw himself living in Atlanta and then in the cottage in the mountains. In each scene he revisited, he knew not only what *he* thought and felt, but also what every other person involved thought and felt.

Many of the scenes were similar. They showed times Mellen had helped people and times he could have helped but hadn't. He saw every stranded motorist he'd ever passed on the side of the road. Though he'd stopped and offered his share of help, there were many more people he hadn't helped. Each time he revisited these scenes, he felt the fear and abandonment that the stranded drivers had felt, standing alone by the side of the road.

He found himself driving along Route 401 in Fayetteville again. It was a hot summer day and the heat made the road ahead look as if it were shimmering. He had just finished a difficult job. It had been a long day, and he was anxious to get home, grab a cold drink from the refrigerator, put his feet up, catch the evening news. Traffic slowed up a bit, and he saw, on the shoulder of the road, a disabled car and a woman looking blankly into its open hood. Someone else will help her. I've helped my share of stranded drivers, Mellen thought. I just want to get home.

Simultaneously, he reexperienced those same moments as the woman. Frustrated, unable to figure out what had gone wrong, she looked at the jumble of wires and cables and valves under the hood, not knowing what it might take to get them all working again. She checked the oil and the antifreeze. Those were fine. She didn't know what else to check. She hoped a police car, or someone who knew about cars, would stop before it got dark. The prospect of being stranded by the road-side in the dark, once rush hour had ended, fright-ened her. But the cars kept skirting past, slowing down only slightly for a look. She was on the verge of tears.

Reliving all these scenes, Mellen felt as all the others who were part of them had felt. Again he understood that he and everyone else were part of a whole, not separate. They were all part of God.

While he relived scenes from his life, he heard voices. They were all talking about him. He was overhearing the thoughts and sharing the feelings of people he'd known. He was hearing and feeling what they'd thought and felt about him. Mellen was astounded by how many people cared deeply for him.

Toward the end, he'd become so embittered that he hadn't seen the good in life, or in many of the people he'd shared it with. He'd never realized un-til he heard these voices. He heard his parents, his brother, his sister, Elizabeth Anne, his grand-parents. There was Susan, and friends, and co-workers from Atlanta. There was Rhonda, his art teacher. And there was his high school friend Bob, someone he'd never considered a particularly good friend. He heard Bob speak of him in the most lov-ing terms, felt the friendship and loyalty Bob had felt for him.

At that moment Mellen realized that any good thought one person had about another, any com-passionate feeling, was enduring. Even if a person was oblivious of the thought, or dismissed the em-pathy at the time, it wasn't wasted. When that per-son was ready, even if this didn't happen until after death, the thought and feeling came back to him or her.

Mellen asked the light to show him what lay beyond. Then he passed into the light itself. The light was every color. He was enveloped by it, a part of it. Then he went through it. As he had seen his life unfold, he saw the history of the cosmos unfold.

He began traveling at an incredible speed away from the Earth. When he'd traveled a vast distance, he saw it, a blue-and-white marbleized ball floating in black space. It looked as it had in the first photos Mellen had seen of Earth from the moon, photos shot by the Apollo astronauts. As he continued to speed into the distance, he watched time roll backward.

The white streaks of cloud that were shot through the blue of the Earth's oceans began to fade. The blue began to disappear as well. Mellen was seeing the Earth as it had looked 3.6 billion years earlier. It was a brownish red. A hard crust of solid earth had just formed at its surface from molten rock below.

Mellen continued to travel outward, and the present receded further. The Earth was now a glowing red. He was seeing it as it had been nearly four billion years earlier, still sorting itself into layers. Molten nickel-iron was settling to the center of the Earth, surrounded by an outer core of liquid nickel-iron, and red, molten rock that bubbled at the surface.

As he traveled still farther out and back in time, Mellen watched the Earth shrink. Over the course of the previous seven hundred million years, the Earth had been growing progressively larger as meteorites had pummeled it surface, drawn in by Earth's gravity. In the light of the sun—newly collapsed under its own gravity and now so hot and bright that it illuminated the solar system—Mellen watched as the meteorites flew away from the Earth. Time continued to roll backward, and Earth was reduced to a clump of solid particles. These had collided with one another to form the planet. Now they too flew apart.

From a vantage point ten billion years in the past, Mellen watched as the processes that had created the Milky Way reversed themselves. The matter that had formed the sun flew apart, and the solar system dimmed. As the particles dispersed, the galaxy spread into a flat, disk-shaped cloud of matter. The disk began to spin, dispersing more and more. By now there was nothing out there but a far-flung cloud of hydrogen and other elemental particles. The cloud was still somewhat condensed, but then Mellen saw it spread out even farther.

For a while there wasn't much to see. The universe was a scattered expanse of particles, mostly hydrogen and helium. It was dark. Going still farther back in time, Mellen observed as space became illuminated. The universe was filled with light, radiation from a gigantic cosmic explosion—the Big Bang.

As events led backward to the Big Bang, the universe continued to shrink. Space, matter and energy contracted and grew hotter. Suddenly everything was part of a great fireball. There was a sound, like a hiss.

Ahead, Mellen saw a second light, thinner but even more powerful than the first light he had crossed through. It was unending. He went through this light and found himself in a void. He knew then that he had traveled back before the Big Bang. There was nothing to see. He understood that the void was nothing but pure consciousness. Mellen sensed that here, in the void, he had access to all information, all knowledge. But there was no way to apply it. Everything that made up the universe had contracted to a minute point. There was no room for anything to happen.

For the first time, Mellen understood that he would be returning to life. He understood the purpose of life. As he understood it then, life was God exploring God's self. Life was God exploring all the permutations and possibilities of all creation. Together, all things and all possibilities were God. Without experience, without the opportunity for events to transpire, there was no exploration. The prospect of returning to life thrilled him.

As soon as it had occurred to Mellen that he would be returning to life, time began to rush forward again. He left the void and began speeding forward in time.

Mellen passed back into the first light. He knew he would be returning to life, and he asked the light if he could bring something back with him. He sensed then that he had access to a wealth of information, all knowledge, but had to choose among what was there. He couldn't bring it all back with him. All sorts of information was at his fingertips—information about the future, about technology, about science. He decided what information he wanted access to, and then he felt himself leave the light.

"Oh, God, I love my life," he said as he left.

And he heard the words the moment he found himself back in his bed again.

∞

CHAPTER FOURTEEN

Kathy Latrelle

Kathy Latrelle was sitting on the set, waiting for the commercial break to end. When it did, they'd be appearing live across America. *Larry King Live* had a wide audience.

The break ended and they were on.

Larry King asked Kathy if she thought she was especially sensitive to psychic or spiritual events. He suggested that she might be a candidate to join the nineteen million Americans who claim UFO sightings or the ten million who report near-death experiences. He mentioned a new book which argues that the two phenomena may be linked and certain people are much more likely to face them.

Larry King was talking about Ken Ring's new book, *The Omega Project*, which included interviews with Kathy and dozens of other near-death experiencers. Kathy wasn't sure she agreed with Ring's premise that UFO sightings and near-death experiences were related.

According to the book, people who'd had troubled childhoods were somewhat more likely than others to have NDEs and contact with UFOs. Kathy wasn't sure about UFOs, period. But she could vouch for near-death experiences, which she knew were real enough. So when Ken asked her to appear on the show with him, she said she'd be glad to.

She and Ken had been friends ever since she'd heard him lecture at Johnson Memorial Hospital in 1986, the same hospital where Tommy Golden had been revived. Two weeks before the lecture, she'd read, scarcely believing what she'd stumbled across, an article about NDEs that he had written for *Connecticut* magazine. It wasn't until she'd read the piece that she realized the experience she'd had in 1979, the experience that had changed her life in so many ways, was something other people had been through too.

She'd taken a day off from her job—she was working as an X-ray technician at Pratt and Whitney Aircraft—to hear Ken lecture. He told her later that he'd picked her out of the audience right off the bat and fingered her for an NDE, the term he'd coined for people who'd had near-death experiences.

That was six years ago. Since then, they'd talked about her experience many times. Ken had answered her questions and asked a lot of his own, some strange ones here and there. "Do you think the NDE changed the organic makeup of your brain?" he once wanted to know. The answer was, as far as she knew, that it hadn't.

Sometimes the two of them goofed around, talked about relationships, sex, whatever. Sometimes Steve Price would join them. Ken had introduced Kathy to the support group for near-death experiencers that Bruce Greyson headed. That was where she met Steve. She and Steve would speak to students in Ken's classes at the university. They'd describe their NDEs and what had happened since. They had a lot of fun. She enjoyed talking to the kids in Ken's class.

For the show today, Ken was going to talk about his new book and she was going to talk about her NDE. Cable News Network, which broadcast *Larry King Live*, flew her to Washington, where the show was filmed.

Ken Ring told the audience that special people may represent the next stage in human evolution. He spoke live from a studio in San Francisco. In Washington, they were joined by UFO researcher Ellen Crystal and Kathy Latrelle.

When Larry King had introduced himself to Kathy, just before the show, he'd struck her as an odd character. He looked odd. It was the big, square black glasses on his nose. The gigantic forehead. The pointy chin that she knew from TV. This guy's so weird, how'd he get married six times? Kathy was thinking while the makeup man did her hair, which she still wore long and parted in the middle. King had interviewed presidents, prostitutes, criminals, crown princes, movie stars, movers and shakers of all kinds. His show was tops in the ratings.

None of that by itself particularly impressed Kathy. It would have intimidated her at one time, but she wasn't the least bit nervous now. Here I am, going on this show with this geeky guy, she'd been thinking in the greenroom. Watching King interview Ken, though, she was impressed. King had a real presence. He was intense, interested. She respected that.

Turning to her after finishing a conversation

with the UFO researcher, King asked Kathy to describe her twenty-fifth birthday.

"On my twenty-fifth birthday, I had a minor operation," Kathy said, remembering the day vividly. "Someone botched up something with the anesthesia. I started to aspirate and suddenly pulled out of my body. I went up. The perspective was from the corner of the operating suite. And I looked down at everything that was going on down there below and I said, 'Wow!' I was in the light."

King wanted to know what that meant.

"I was in the light of love, God, eternity, whatever you want to call it," she began. And she found, as she always did, that when she thought or talked about being in the light, she felt she was there again. There was that overwhelming, transforming sense of being loved, accepted, belonging, no strings attached. It was a feeling she'd never had until she died, and now it never left her.

"I was within this wonderful, loving, beautiful, incredible, indescribable light. And I looked down at that and I said, 'Well, it's my twenty-fifth birthday and I'm going to die, and who cares? It's really nice up here!' "

King was looking at her intently. He asked her how she knew all of this wasn't some sort of hallucination—a question people often asked—and she tried to explain.

"It has an entirely different feel," she replied. "The depth of it was incredible. It changed me completely and I did not even acknowledge that it had happened. And yet, simply, that five minutes changed my entire life so much that there's—I mean, it was—there's no way that it could be any kind of hallucination."

King then asked Ken whether he believed Kathy had actually experienced what she described, and Ken said yes, he was convinced she had.

For one thing, the way she spoke about the experience had convinced him. It was her sincerity, her earnestness. She clearly wasn't trying to impress anyone. There was nothing self-aggrandizing in the way she described her experience. "If I hadn't gone in for surgery that morning, I don't think I was destined to get hit by a truck so I would have this experience," she'd told him. "It just happened. Shit luck." She laughed.

There was always that element of humor. She was a very funny woman. Ken also remembered that she'd told him she sensed there was a wall behind her when she was in the light. Always clumsy, she worried she'd fall backward. "I was afraid I'd trip into eternity," she'd told him, laughing again.

The other thing that had convinced Ken was the way she loved those boys, absolutely unconditionally, completely unselfishly. She'd been caring for the youngest since he was born, and now he was eight or nine. For someone who had been abandoned as regularly as she had when she was growing up, it was incredible that she was taking that risk. The boys weren't hers. They weren't even related to her. If Ken remembered right, the boys were the nephews of a friend. Their parents cared for them in a haphazard way and Kathy had more or less been filling in the gaps. They stayed with her during weekends and sometimes during the week. She paid for their doctors' visits and their clothes, and took them places.

All the same, she had no legal rights to them. There was never any guarantee that their parents would agree to let her have them from one weekend to the next, or that they wouldn't pull up stakes and move. Still, Kathy didn't seem to find anything heroic or even noteworthy in this. Clearly, something had changed her life in a profound way, Ken thought.

It wasn't that the circumstances of her life had changed that much, though. She was still living in the same place, still working in a hospital, though now as a nurse. But she had changed. The kind of person she was had changed, and so had her outlook. You had to remind yourself that she had the upbringing she'd had. In some ways she was the same person she'd been at twenty-five—a down-to-earth, tell-it-to-me-straight-I'm-no-fool type—but with a self-confidence and warmth and generosity that were extraordinary.

King also wanted to know if Kathy had a troubled childhood.

"I suppose you could say it was dysfunctional," she told him.

Did that make her more sensitive to experiences like NDEs? he asked. And she said she thought it could. She could see the good things that had come out of her experiences as a child. In part, the NDE had helped her do that. And it had helped her move on.

King addressed the next question to the UFO researcher. The conversation turned to talk of extraterrestrial and UFO sightings. Then King had a final question for Kathy.

Was she glad the event took place?

"Absolutely."

* * *

And she was. She was, even though things were very, very bad after the NDE. Everything fell apart. The real changes, the ones for the better, didn't show up for a couple of years.

In the beginning, it was confusing, frightening at times. So many things happened so fast, she was barely able to sort them out, let alone understand what had gone on in the operating suite.

One of the reasons it was so hard to sort out what had happened was that no one wanted her to talk about it. While she was still in the hospital recovery room, Kathy started telling the nurses she had floated up to the ceiling and found herself bathed in this miraculous, healing light.

"It's the drugs, hon," they told her, bending closer, peering into her face, giving her pulse an extra check and patting her hand. "Good drugs. You'll feel fine after you get some rest."

The same thing happened when Kathy tried to tell her mother about the experience. "You need rest,' her mother said. It happened again when she told the people at the doctor's office where she was working as an X-ray technician.

From the start, she never felt she fit in at the office. She felt the same way she had in school and in the Air Force. In retrospect, she realized it was a mistake to tell the people at work. Judging from what happened after, they must have thought she was crazy.

After trying to explain to the nurses, then her mother, then at the office, Kathy stopped trying. She figured what had happened was the result of hypoxia, insufficient oxygen to the brain.

I know I died, she thought. *It's so bizzarre. I wonder if this ever happened to anyone else. If it* did, though, wouldn't we have heard about it by now?

She had no idea what to make of the feeling she'd had in the light. Just thinking about it was an overwhelming experience. It had been a rapturous feeling, unlike any she had ever had. In the light, she'd felt completely accepted and loved. She decided that, for the time being, she wouldn't think about it. She'd concentrate on getting back on her feet, back into the routine.

At the time, she was renting a house in Meriden, a few towns east of Waterbury and very much like it. Alan was still in Turkey. It was just she and the dogs.

Her place wasn't far from where her mother and Ted lived, and Kathy visited them every now and then after work. She spent one weekend a month drilling with her Air Force Reserve unit; other weekends she rode with the Sand and River County Riders, a dirt-bike riders' club. She had a Suzuki GS1100 road bike, which she took to work. But her dirt bike, a Can Am 175, was her love.

There were a lot of nice people in the club, a lot of different people—lawyers, architects, cops, businessmen. She enjoyed those weekends. After all the hours at work, it was a relief to get on her bike and hit the gas, feel the dirt grind up under the wheels, fly through the green tunnel-like paths between the trees, forget everything else.

One particularly cold day after her surgery, Kathy got a phone call at home. It was Doris, her father's second wife. In actual fact, they hadn't married, but they'd been together longer than many married couples Kathy knew, for ten years.

"Kathy? It's Doris. I'm calling because your

daddy, uh, Kathy? Your daddy—" Doris started sobbing before she could finish.

She didn't have to finish. Kathy had been expecting this call for weeks. The doctors had pretty much given up on her father. Now, at fifty-three, he was dead.

Goddammit, Kathy thought. Here it is, Daddy and I just start to talk, and he starts to turn into a decent parent, and now he's gone. Why couldn't he have done this before, when he was healthy? Why'd he have to smoke himself to death?

Eventually, Doris calmed down enough to tell Kathy she'd have to come down to Florida to identify her father's body. Since she and Kathy's father weren't legally married, Doris couldn't do it herself. Only a legal relative could.

She knew it was a long way from Connecticut to Florida, and that Kathy had just been sick, Doris said. But she couldn't think of anyone else to ask. They hadn't heard from Lloyd in months and didn't know where he was. And, of course, Kathy's mother couldn't come.

So Kathy arranged for a week off from work and booked a flight. She was fired just before her flight. Kathy was completely thrown off-balance. For a moment she wasn't sure what had happened. Had they really just fired her like that? She'd just lost her father. Now she was losing her job? How was she going to get by? Why couldn't things work out?

She wanted to sit down, to think. But she couldn't get hold of a thought. There was no place or time to sit and get her bearings, anyway. She had to catch a plane at Bradley Airport in ninety minutes.

Without registering any of the signposts along

the way, she drove there. She felt humiliated and hurt. She'd have three hours in the air, she thought as a skycap reached for her bags. Maybe she could figure something out. Until they took off, at least, she just didn't want to think about anything.

Powder Ridge was a ski resort in Middlefield, not far from Waterbury. It didn't offer world-class skiing. It was the kind of place where families went skiing. The slopes weren't too dangerous, so the kids didn't get hurt. There was a lodge with a restaurant at the foot of the slopes where you could get hot dogs and hamburgers and tuna sandwiches. That was where Kathy got a job, making sandwiches, after she returned from Florida.

The job at the resort wasn't what she'd hoped for when she opened the paper to the Help Wanted section her first day back. But there weren't any openings for X-ray techs. Identifying her father had been rough. She was anxious to get back to work. And all told, the job wasn't that bad. She wasn't going to sulk.

"I have a lot of respect for you, Kathy," Ted told her one day, stopping by after work, taking her by surprise. He had never paid her a compliment before. "You've never been without a job, and I respect that. You haven't just been sitting around whining like some people might."

She had always seemed such a hellion, Ted thought. But now he was seeing her in a new light. From where she stood, Kathy didn't see that she had many choices. Alan was still in Turkey. She had to support herself.

"If I sat around whining, that'd be as bad as if

I hit myself in the face with a hammer," Kathy told Ted that day. But she appreciated the compliment. She appreciated Ted now too. She still didn't like the way he treated her mother, but that was between her mother and Ted. He treated *her* well and they had a good relationship. Her relationship with her mother continued to improve as well.

A few months passed and she realized one morning, while making another sandwich for another skier and looking out the window, that losing her job hadn't been entirely a bad thing. If nothing else, it had helped bring her and Ted and her mother closer.

It was strange, she thought. She felt calmer than she ever had, far more calm than she would have imagined under the circumstances. Here she was, making her umpteenth sandwich of the day, in a dead-end job, with no security, no husband, no house. Yet she could see something valuable that had come out of the situation.

If the bad things in your life can teach you a lesson, they aren't necessarily all that bad, she thought. Bad stuff happens to everyone, but if you turn it into something positive, and learn from it, then it's not necessarily bad.

In part, she attributed this change in outlook to maturity. But she began to wonder if it didn't also have something to do with the strange thing that had happened that day in the OR. The feeling she'd had in the light that day—that feeling of complete acceptance, of being loved so completely—had returned. It was the feeling, she told Ken later, of being with God. Now she almost always felt that way.

If someone had told her two years earlier that

she'd feel this way, she would have broken up.
She hadn't believed there was a God. "God is a
manifestation of man's need to have something to
believe in," she'd say. She'd still go to church
every now and then, but more out of habit than
anything. It brought back happy memories of the
Sundays she'd spent at the Methodist church as a
little girl. But she stopped going to church alto-
gether after she married Alan. He never went.

She'd begun to notice other changes in herself
since the day in the OR. Some odd ones. Her
taste in music, for starters. She'd always hated the
classical music her parents had played at home in
Waterbury. She liked rock—Uriah Heep, the
Beach Boys, the Beatles. But after that day in surgery, she couldn't hear enough Mozart. It reminded her vaguely of the music she'd heard in
the light.

At the same time, she began to feel this over-
riding, and surprising, desire to go to school. Before, she'd never wanted to bother. Now she
desperately wanted to go to college. She knew
she'd always had the potential. She was still trying to decide where to go, and what to study,
when she heard from Alan. He was coming home
from Turkey.

Kathy had missed Alan terribly when he'd left
for Turkey. She'd longed for him. But those feelings had faded somewhat. It had been two years,
after all. She wasn't as happy to hear he was
coming home as she'd expected. It seemed now,
as she remembered him, that they had never had
very much in common and had even less in common now. In part, she realized, she had married
Alan out of fear. Everyone else got married.
There was a lot of pressure to get married too.

Maybe she'd caved in to that. For some reason, fear didn't get the better of her the way it once had.

Still, she was fond of Alan. She cared about him and, in a different way now, she loved him. She agreed to let him move in.

"You're different," Alan said one afternoon after she'd had a disagreement with someone over the phone. Instead of blowing up the way she used to, she'd simply written the person a letter, Alan noticed. "You'd have torn them apart before," he said. And she would have. But she didn't feel like blowing up that way any longer.

"I used to be angry all the time. I had a heck of a time in the service because I think they detected that anger, this defiance," she told Ken Ring later. "Before the NDE, I was off-balance almost all the time. It didn't take much to throw off the whole apple cart. If I picked up a jar of jelly by the top, and it fell to the floor, that was a big deal. I really got P.O.'d. Now I just get the paper towels and wipe it up. Before, little stuff bothered me. Alan still gets bothered by things like that. Things freak him out."

One of the things that bothered Alan was Kathy's attempts to talk about what happened in the operating room, and also her plan to go to college. He wouldn't listen to her talk about the former and he wasn't much better about the latter.

"You don't need that. You don't need school," he'd say whenever the subject came up.

To avoid arguments, Kathy dropped plans for school. But only temporarily. It didn't take her long to realize that the problem she and Alan had had in Omaha was a problem in Meriden. She was too independent for him. And now there were even more things she wanted to do. School was one of those things. Finally, she asked Alan to leave.

CHAPTER FIFTEEN

ॐ

Kate Valentine

It's late afternoon and an acrid cold rattles your bones as you duck between two white buildings and into the rear door of Kate Valentine's painting studio. This is snow country. Bitter winds sweep south into valley communities like this one in western Connecticut and chill your soul. The smell of wood-burning stoves and fireplaces fills the air.

There's already been more than one northeaster this season, the kind of foul weather you thought existed only in adventure novels. In fact, record-low temperatures make this New England winter especially difficult. Six years and counting until the end of the century, and people are already betting that this season will make it into the history books.

But the conversation inside Kate's place is warm. And for those who come here with other things weighing on their minds, it is comforting, even if they arrive under the guise of learning how to paint. The painting is part of what everyone clearly does here. But the music and feelings in this room transcend what you might find in any other craft class. Coming here to paint got Anita through the last months of chemo, her daughter says. It really helps her forget the cancer that is slowly killing her and the treatments that bring about a very sad kind of sickness all its own.

Carol chews gum and ducks outside occasionally to smoke, even in this weather. Looking like someone raised on acid rock or the hillbilly stuff Kate herself was raised on, Carol sinks into the cadence of the baroque music played in this place. Although these classes are not advertised, students seem to find their way to the studio to paint another bentwood basket or mixe milk paints into authenticate hues. Many of the people seated around the table are regulars, though some have perfected techniques that would allow them to go off on their own if they wished to leave Kate.

Many of the scenes these people paint could have come from the countryside just outside the studio windows. Some of the barns depicted in the sometimes flat, sometimes three-dimensional works are still standing. Street scenes are scenes not too hard to find up and down the road. The only noticeable difference is the cars and traffic lights left out of the paintings.

The studio has been open only since November, and although students have been coming here for just three months, their work has taken on a finished look to distinguish it from Kate's own work.

No one asks the hard questions. Talk around the table is limited to technique and colors, not the life-and-death stuff Kate used to talk about in her television interviews. When she is asked by visitors whether or not God exists, she fields these questions with the good grace of someone who has never claimed to know everything.

What Kate does know is highly personal and

spiritual. She has faith in what she knows in the same way a priest exhibits faith in the church. But she is a freelance person of God, as she likes to say. And practices her faith while she paints, talks, makes coffee or does any of the other ordinary things she does.

Kate does not have faith in the Catholic Church which raised her. But she does have a kind of reverence for people who still need that kind of faith, and she does not ridicule even the staunchest dogma. She just cannot embrace it any longer as absolute truth.

Her faith, she says, stems from the time she spent in the light, and she attributes it to any clarity she now enjoys regarding life, liberty and a never-ending pursuit of happiness.

Like the others, Kate still has unanswered questions. At will, she says, she can ask these questions by simply returning to the light. There, she says, she can again find her authentic self.

"It's like getting rid of a skin, and everything that seemed important, you realize isn't important. I saw mountains, valleys, water and the color green on a scale that I've never encountered," Kate says, brushing back her closely cropped gray hair.

"I don't know if it had something to do with the purity of the light, but the colors were so intense." She stares off into some distant place. Outside, it is getting dark and gray shadows creep up along the sides of the whitewashed buildings.

As she talks, Kate is clearly lost again in the memory of that first time she spent in the light. Actually, remembering it does not exactly describe what sometimes happens, she says. Like others, Kate says she can reexperience the light, an ability that could never be equaled by a mere memory of such an experience.

For her, that first time was a humbling experience, one that allowed her to relive her own shortcomings and learn instantly that it was okay.

"I was incredibly sorry for things I had done, instantly sorry," she said. "I got an instant sense that it doesn't matter, from this paternal wave of love that kind of washes over you." She was standing on that high mountain, looking down into a valley.

"At that moment I knew that if I went down to the valley, I could stay. I wanted to run, this was it, and I became aware of the children at home and my husband, Paul, and I knew they'd be all right. But then I was told I had to go back. I was fighting to stay, but it didn't do me any good."

And then she had a revelation.

"I understood the incredible power that we are all empowered with," she said. "And I understood that our thoughts have far-reaching effects. To come into that power, though," she said, pausing, "you have to have absolute control over your thoughts, because they can literally destroy."

She speaks slowly now, but lightly, trying to explain herself in concrete ways in order to be fully understood. Her dog nestles closer. The music in the studio plays somber stuff, then lighter, happier arrangements without interrupting either the mood or the points she's trying to emphasize now as we talk.

"We are all the source," she says. "We are gods. We keep looking outside ourselves, but we are all interconnected to all things. We are really one with the earth, the air, the animals and each other. It's an illusion that there is separateness. We don't want to know it, though, because then we have a responsibility to everything around us, and we don't want to know."

Kate no longer does the television circuit of interviews, and shies away from any direct publicity. In fact, the interviews for this book took place over a period of weeks and she was always guarded about her privacy.

"I am doing this interview because I don't think people understand just how important the changes after an NDE are, and nobody has fully explored it yet," she said.

"It's not automatic. It takes work, and a lot of people who have had this experience pay far too much attention to the NDE, when it's what happens afterwards that is really important."

Ken Ring has also taken a step back from the spotlight, even though producers from some of the most popular television shows still call the university looking for him. Ken screens his calls but is polite enough to enlist the help of others still interested in telling their own stories.

Neither Kate or Ken has become reclusive, but both seem bent on focusing on some new path these experiences have led them to explore.

Kate lives to paint now. It's her quiet way of tapping into the experience of a lifetime.

"The paintings that I do may be my way of sharing a very simplistic place, and maybe if people look at it, they can access it too," she says, repeating a claim she and others like her have often expressed.

People can tap into their own experiences too if they choose, and emerge as Kate, Kathy and the others have, changed in fundamental ways. This is what they believe.

"That place is accessible to me anytime," Kate says. "I just get very quiet and let it come to me. I have faith, and there's no better word for it, and it fills you up," she says, almost whispering.

"I feel the peace, an all-pervasive peace. It's not as intense as I felt it the first time, but I think that's because we're not wired in this dimension to receive it directly.

"But I can receive it enough to allow me to access the next important step, the faith that I need . . ."

Like Ken, Kate also believes that NDEs are not new, but merely the subject of more rapid and thorough communications. A television program that might have been seen only in Chicago by a few million people can now by syndicated worldwide and seen by tens of millions in the same year. This alone has created a tumbling, snowball effect that has catapulted the NDE into the forefront of people's minds.

But, they also believe this publicity comes at a critical time in human history.

"People need to get simple again," says Kate, who now eats only locally grown vegetables because she says they vibrate at the same rate that she vibrates. By eating foods that vibrate at the same rate, Kate says she stays in balance. This balance helps keep her attuned to her surroundings, she claims.

"People do have access to a higher, evolutionary plane. That's where I think we [NDErs] are, harbingers of what people will be like in the next hundred years or so," she says, speaking confidently.

She says the so-called baby boomer generation—people born between the late 1940s and the early

1960s—is aging now and beginning to think about its own mortality.

"They're going to have to start thinking about what happens after this life," she says, and to find the answer, they're going to have to find a new spirituality "that most of us have never encountered before."

To make the shift, Kate says people will have to begin their own transformations.

"There are some physical things you can do," she says, careful to point out there is no single formula for achieving a higher consciousness. But she observes that there are environmental blocks that may prevent people from finding levels of peace possible for them now.

"Television, the newspaper, it's all negative, so get it out of your life," she says.

This is a first step, Kate believes, toward cleansing your intake of information that often serves no useful purpose. "There will come a time when you can handle it, but you've been desensitized.

"Don't read the newspaper for six weeks. When you pick it up, you're going to be a new person. Don't watch TV or movies during this period. Be very careful what you put into your mind," she cautions. "You won't miss anything, because people will make sure you know what's going on.

"But this is a personal journey, and you have to learn to stop people from telling you their negative thoughts. Stop people from dumping on you," says this woman who years earlier had learned to tune out an abusive family by reading and listening to classical music. "I think I learned at an early age to turn inward," she says now.

Next, she says, your diet influences you in ways seldom associated with food.

"Try to eat only things that are grown locally," she advises, because "they vibrate at the same rate you vibrate. When you go to the supermarket, don't buy Florida-grown vegetables. Stay away from any form of meat and fish. The fish is filled with chemicals from the water."

She pauses in the middle of this menu, saying, "I know this sounds strict." But she continues, telling us our foods are filled with stimulants, compounds and undetermined substances which make a daily cocktail of things our bodies do not use naturally.

"Stay with the grains and rice. These things seemed to be okay no matter where they're grown. Stay away from sugar. Honey is okay, especially if it is local. Finally, drink lots of water and never use caffeine."

All of this, she says, is a way of fine-tuning your receiver.

How well any of this will work depends upon how far people are willing to take it.

"Take all of the things I've given you and you'll find all levels of personal empowerment," says Kate, whose students include a number of cancer patients. And while she says some come to the studio to find sympathy and mourn their own passing, others come just to quietly draw and paint with Kate, not to talk about their illnesses.

"If you practice, you find that thinking can be a powerful source of energy," she says. In the 1920s, the economy was depressed and so were people. "This collective negative thinking caused sandstorms. In the Reagan era, the economy wasn't good but we believed that it was, and when he left, it collapsed."

"You have the ability to call people into your

life who have the same type of hunger. Find them," she says "and collectively, you have the power . . . to affect the world around you physically."

In *Illusion* by Richard Bach, he tells the story of a wonderful manuscript that has all the answers in the world in it.

"You have to read the book, put it aside, and whatever you are meant to glean from it, you are meant to learn," Kate says.

She is talking about this book and her own NDE.

❧

CHAPTER SIXTEEN

Kathy Latrelle

Members of Kathy's Air Force Reserve unit—bankers, lawyers, machinists, X-ray techs and housewives in their civilian lives—met at an oil-stained airstrip one weekend a month to prepare for whatever occasions might prompt the President to "call up the reserves." By 1982, Kathy had been in the reserves only a year.

She liked the reserves. She thought it was important. And it offered certain fringe benefits. The Air Force paid tuition at any public university you chose. And Kathy was determined to go back to school. Now that she was on her own again—Alan had moved out, at her request—there was nothing holding her back.

As it turned out, the military provided a far bigger benefit than free tuition. It was through the Air Force that Kathy had met Donald, and through him, the boys.

Donald was a nice guy. Kathy liked him. When he suggested one day that she go with him to visit his sister, she agreed.

Donald's sister, Darlene, lived nearby. The couple had two children. Kathy had never liked children. She'd never had patience for them. But that had begun to change. She found she had a lot more patience all around.

Still, Kathy was completely taken by surprise by Norman, Darlene's five-year-old. He was a charmer, happy, outgoing and funny. His little brother, two-year-old Chris, was also a charmer, just a little more shy. They went to see the old Deep River Fife and Drum Corps muster, and had a great time together.

Things at home were a little rough for the kids. Neither Darlene nor her husband worked. They got by on welfare. Sometimes they didn't pay as much attention to the kids as they needed to. When the time came for Donald and Kathy to leave that first day, Norman wouldn't let Kathy go. Darlene ended up sending him home with her.

And that was how it began. Nearly every weekend after, except the weekends she was drilling with the reserves, Kathy would drive to Darlene's, chat for a while, then take Norman for the weekend.

Kathy and Norman would go for bike rides. They'd read stories together. They built a toy box for his "stuff," which had started accumulating. On trips to the store to get him shoes and socks and warm sweaters, she hadn't been able to resist buying him toys. Norman made friends with the neighborhood kids. After a year had passed, Chris demanded to be taken as well.

Kathy couldn't remember why she'd always found children irritating. She found just the opposite now. Norman and Chris were absolutely joyous, so excited and excitable, so enthusiastic, so funny, so personable, so open, so loving. The three of them would pile into her Jeep and head to the Monster Truck show to eat blue cotton candy and pink hot dogs, and to fling themselves out of their seats and scream when the giant pickups mowed over the tiny compact cars. They had Nintendo contests, each trying to accumulate more points in Super Mario Brothers than the others. They raced tiny remote-controlled cars. They had a ball together.

They had a ball together, but Kathy always made it clear the boys had to behave themselves. There were no excuses for fighting, for goofing off and running into trouble at school, for neglecting to be polite. She wanted the boys to get along with other people, to know how to carry themselves, to learn, to do well.

In the fall of 1982, Kathy decided she couldn't wait any longer to go back to school. She took courses at nearby Middlesex Community College. Because she was a member of the Air Force National Guard, and because Middlesex was a public school, tuition was free. And it was better than she'd expected. Like Kathy, most of the students at Middlesex had been out of high school for a few years and were holding down jobs and commuting to campus. Kathy felt comfortable. She still found it hard to sit still in class, but she was determined to finish. When she heard she could get credit for the X-ray training she'd had in the Air Force National Guard, she decided to major in X-ray technology.

Weekdays she'd get up, walk the dogs, grab some breakfast and drive to Pratt and Whitney. After work she'd head to school, then back home. Every fourth weekend of the month she'd drill with her National Guard unit. The rest of her weekends were for the boys.

Six months after Kathy first met them, Darlene had another baby, another boy, who was named Paul. Darlene sent the baby home with Kathy the next day. With Paul, Kathy went through all the new parent's late-night feedings, inexplicable bouts of crying and fearful trips to the doctor for ear infections and measles scares. This was only on the weekends, but it was enough.

The boys became the most important thing in Kathy's life.

They came first. If she had plans with a friend, or her mother or Ted, or Alan—with whom she'd finally become friends—she'd cancel to be with the boys. She went without things—her vintage Chevy truck sat in the yard, rusting for lack of attention—so the boys could get regular checkups and trips to the dentist and coats and sneakers and books to read and toys to play with.

There were three ten-inch stacks of Nintendo games on top of the living room TV; the toy box was jammed full of Matchbox cars, and arts and crafts kits, and puzzles. Board games were tottering atop books on the bookshelves. When the kids wanted to see Disney World, Kathy took them all to Florida.

It wasn't that Kathy did these things out of obligation. She simply didn't want to do things any differently. She wanted the boys to have a stable place with her, and all the things other kids had. She couldn't have chosen not to care so much. She loved the boys, no strings attached.

Kathy knew she had no legal right to see them from one weekend to the next. Darlene could change her mind, decide Kathy couldn't see them, and that would be the end of it all. At one time in Kathy's life, that would have been more than enough reason for her not to get involved. She knew she was taking a risk. But that wasn't the important thing. The important thing was that the boys needed her.

Now and then, Kathy would think about what happened in the operating room that day back in 1979. That feeling she'd had in the light—that feeling of being accepted and loved absolutely—had come back to her over and over since then. Then it began to linger. Now she felt all the time.

It wasn't until Kathy read Ken's article about NDEs in *Connecticut* magazine, though, that she realized there was a name for what she'd been through, and that other people had been through the very same thing. After reading the article, she'd gone to hear Ken speak at Johnson Memorial Hospital.

"You've had a near-death experience, haven't you?" Ken asked when she introduced herself after the lecture. They talked a while and exchanged phone numbers. Ken also gave Kathy the number for the IANDS support group in Hartford.

That was how she got to know Ken and Bruce and Steve. Bruce headed the support-group meetings. And Steve attended most of them. Kathy liked the meetings. Though she felt at ease with most people, there were some things only members of the group could understand, like how much an NDE could change you.

Some in the group were having a really rough time adjusting after their experiences. The others offered support and advice. An NDE can change your life, Kathy would tell other NDErs. But you had to work at it.

She had to take what the NDE had taught her and go from there. And it wasn't always easy. But things did work out.

"I guess I don't put as much weight on my NDE as other people," she told Ken Ring." I give it weight, but not exclusively. I changed because I had the NDE, but I also changed because I matured. People change all the time."

The next big change came when she decided to go back to school. It was 1987. The boys were getting older—and Kathy wanted to spend more time with them. Her schedule at Pratt and Whitney made that virtually impossible except on weekends. She finished work when the boys were already asleep. She knew nurses were enough in demand that she could dictate her hours.

So she enrolled as a full-time nursing student at Quinnipiac College. It was a grind, much tougher than the first time around. After working at Pratt and Whitney all day, she'd spend most of the night in class. Sometimes she had to take Ritalin again.

In the summer of 1993, Kathy graduated with her nursing degree. She'd already been offered a job at a city hospital. And she was good at her job, patient and empathetic. The other nurses noticed it.

"You never lose your patience, do you?" one said, soon after she'd started on a bad afternoon when they had more than the usual number of temperamental patients and doctors on their hands.

Kathy rarely did lose her patience, even with Norman, with whom she was starting to have some problems. In 1993, he turned fifteen, which was a hard age under the best of circumstances. Norman's weren't. His folks were still a little haphazard with their parenting, by Kathy's standards.

Norman had started stealing. Kathy had caught

him at it several times. Finally she told him he'd have to stop coming over until he cleaned up his act.

"You know, Darlene could decide someday that you can't have the boys anymore, Kathy," her mother reminded her one afternoon a few months later.

Her mother had stopped by for lunch, and was waiting in the kitchen while Kathy made baked macaroni and cheese. Kathy's mother had been worrying aloud about what Darlene might do since Kathy had met the boys, nearly thirteen years now. Well, that was her mother, Kathy thought.

But she was more worried than usual now that Norman had stopped coming over. Kathy's mother was particularly fond of Norman, who loved traveling as much as she did and had recently become her traveling companion. Kathy's mother missed him and had begun to worry that one day she'd find herself cut off from all three boys, whom she'd come to regard as grandchildren.

But Chris, now thirteen, and Paul, ten, were easier than Norman. They were still in those halcyon days of childhood, or as close as they could get, considering the problems they had at home.

They were outside at the moment, playing with the neighbors' kids. They'd dragged their bicycles through the mud of an early winter thaw, down the road to the lake near Kathy's house. They both got along well with other kids, Kathy noticed. They were funny, and they were good talkers, especially Chris.

"We brought all the bikes back," Chris said, pushing through the back door into the kitchen. Two of the neighbors' kids had gone down to the lake with Paul and Chris, and neither of the two had bicycles. So Chris found two extras among the bikes Kathy had collected over the years. In almost any group, Chris ended up the leader. He was a good-looking kid, with a squared-off face, light brown hair and brown eyes. He had a lot of self-confidence. And he was very bright. He was already talking about college; at the moment, he wanted to go to Georgetown.

Paul followed Chris in. "You wanna go out?" he asked Hawkeye, bending down to give the dog a scratch between the ears. A terrier-poodle-mix mutt, Hawkeye had been hit by a car and blinded. Someone had dumped him at the pound and Kathy had rescued him. Paul loved the dog.

Paul looked just like his older brother, minus a few years. They'd both gotten their hair cut recently. Matching crew cuts, flat on top. Paul wanted to do everything Chris did. He was the quieter of the two. Diagnosed with learning disabilities, he could be shy and unsure of himself at times, but he was getting over that.

They both came in tracking mud, and Kathy stopped them on their way to the living room and made them take off their boots. Not that her place was sterling—she'd had to empty the stove of old McDonald's cups and a shoe box before putting the macaroni in—but she had to draw the line somewhere. She wanted some order in their lives. Kathy knew how hard it was for them because it had been hard for her. She also knew they didn't have to throw in the towel.

"If your life is really bad, you have to look at it and say, 'What is really bad?' and you have to change it," she would tell them over and over, hoping the words would come to mind when they'd need them the most. "If you just hang out and let it happen to you, then it's your fault it's so bad, you stupid fool."

It was hard for Kathy to explain why she invested so much in the boys. Darlene could very well decide one weekend that she couldn't see them anymore. Kathy didn't expect Darlene to do that because they all got along well. But it was a possibility.

Still, it was a risk worth taking. Kathy loved the boys and they needed her. She wasn't going to stay away to protect herself from the prospect of loss.

It was particularly hard to explain this to her mother, who had never been one to take emotional risks. Much as Kathy had grown to love Ted, she knew he hadn't been good for her mother. But her mother had been afraid to give him up because she didn't want to risk being alone.

After years of fighting cancer, Ted had died in 1989. Nearly five years had passed, and her mother still missed him. So did Kathy.

It wasn't until Ted's death that Kathy understood the meaning of one of the glimpses into her future that she'd had in the light. She'd seen her life laid out before her, an illuminated, road. The segments that represented times of joy glowed in beautiful color. Those that represented times of loss and sorrow were black. She'd seen the boys there, in one of the sections that glowed so vibrantly. And she'd seen a black stretch awaiting her in her thirties, but hadn't known just what loss was in store. It was Ted.

When Kathy had made the decision to return from the light, she understood, in a way she never had, that pain was a part of life. Looking at the glowing road that charted the joys and losses in her life, she saw how everything fit together. She'd run into plenty of dark patches before and, each time, struggled to move on and found the way illuminated again. She no longer feared death, or life.

"It's true, Mom," she told her mother, sliding the macaroni and cheese into the now empty oven. "Darlene could decide I can't see the boys. But they know right from wrong and they know who loves them, and if my influence has been positive in their lives, it's worth it. I'd like to think, one day when they're thirty or forty, they'll think, I'm a good man, and I wouldn't be that way if it weren't for Kathy. Then I'll know my life has been worth something, that I've had some good influence on someone."

She hoped Norman would come around soon. I've certainly tried to give him the necessary moral fortitude to do it, she thought.

In the other room, Kathy heard Chris and Paul playing Battleship. They were having some kind of disagreement. She could tell Chris was trying hard not to run out of patience.

"A-Two is a miss? That's impossible, Paul! A-Two can't be a miss. A-One was a hit and you just said B-One was a hit! You're cheating! Kathy! Would you come look at Paul's board—please?"

Kathy came in from the kitchen and looked.

"No one likes to play with a cheater, Paul," she said. He looked hurt. He was so sensitive. "C'mon, let's play Uncle Wiggly," she said, offering a face-saving way out. "That's a better game. You get it down from the shelf."

"I think the NDE is an almost instant form of self-actualization," Kathy says today, summing up.

"The NDE is a way to self-actualization. You get

to the point where you stop doing things for yourself and start doing things for everyone else," she says. "You get to the point where the things you do are for the enrichment of your soul, not your material worth."

∾

CHAPTER SEVENTEEN

Mellen-Thomas Benedict

Mellen felt himself return to his body. He opened his eyes and saw Susan staring down at him in bed.

"You were dead!" Susan said, shocked and frightened. "I know you were dead! You were dead for at least an hour!"

Mellen was so groggy, exhausted and confused that he couldn't answer her.

"I checked your eyes, and your heart and pulse," she said. "You were dead."

"I guess I was," he said, still not entirely sure what had happened to him.

The next three days he stayed in bed. Susan seemed intent on keeping her mind off the possibility that he had actually died and somehow come back to life. The idea frightened her. Since he was still weak and needed her help, she could concentrate on taking care of him. She seemed calmer. But Mellen would catch her looking at him now and then with a look that approached fear.

He knew she was frightened, in fact. That was the strangest thing. He could actually hear her thoughts. Despite herself, she was thinking, over and over, I know he was dead. Mellen could feel how she felt.

By then it had all come back to him—the trip through the light, the faces of the gods, the life review, the jungle, the trip through time and the universe. He had no idea what he was supposed to do next.

After a week, it was clear that he and Susan had to make some preliminary decisions. He'd recovered, or at least gone into remission. In any event, he was able to take care of himself now. Susan didn't have to be there. And Mellen knew she didn't want to be.

They stayed another week. Mellen was still confused, unsure where he was supposed to go from there. Susan made up her mind first. One day she announced that she was going to Florida to see some friends. They were both relieved. Mellen ultimately decided to go back to Fayetteville and reopen the stained-glass shop. Beyond that, he wasn't sure.

"You're certain you're okay?" Susan asked him the morning they locked up the cottage, packed the car and drove to the airport. He reassured her that he was. "I know you died," she said, watching his face.

"I think I did," he told her, hoping the confirmation would be more soothing than a denial. Susan looked confused and somewhat sad.

Not knowing what to say next, they embraced. Mellen thanked her. After Susan went to Florida, they kept in touch sporadically. But when he moved a second time, they lost touch, something he always regretted.

It was warmer in Fayetteville than it had been in

the mountains. Mellen drove to his parents' house, a brick ranch in the suburban outskirts of the city. As far as they knew, he was simply coming home from a six-month hiatus at a friend's vacation home in the mountains. Mellen didn't say anything to the contrary. He explained that he was back from his break, and planned to find a new place to live and reopen his studio.

After some hunting, he found a small house for rent. It was on Yadkin Road, across the street from a small shopping mall. There was a space for lease in the mall as well, and he rented it for his shop.

Though that was settled, Mellen still felt extremely anxious and uncertain. He was trying to sort through what he'd learned in the light, to figure out how he was supposed to live his life. He wasn't even sure just then whether he was cured. Maybe the tumor was still there and he didn't have much more time. Maybe the blackouts would begin again. Maybe something had happened to his brain. Certainly he wasn't his "old self" again.

For one thing, he continued to hear other people's thoughts and to experience their feelings. It was interesting at first. But then it became overwhelming. He was more sensitive to sound in general, and to smells. He was being bombarded with information and sensation.

There was the day he went to the Cross Creek Mall to pick up some supplies. The cacophony was almost deafening. Um, look at those legs! he heard a man, another shopper, think to himself as a teenage girl passed by. I wonder if I could get Helen to buy me that watch, he heard another man think in the jewelry section of a department store. Small children would run by and he'd hear a raucous buzz. Apparently there was nothing but a racket in their heads at times.

With the thoughts he overheard, Mellen experienced the accompanying feelings—lust, desire, anger, confusion. He stopped going to places where he knew he could expect a crowd.

Like his parents, most of Mellen's friends thought he'd simply come back after an extended stay in the mountains. There were a half dozen, though, who knew the real story. And they were almost as shocked as Susan had been when they saw him again. Mellen tried to explain what had happened—the trip through the light and back. If any of his friends were familiar with near-death experiences, that didn't make them anymore accepting. Whenever he brought up the subject, they turned the conversation elsewhere. He knew it made them uncomfortable. He knew they thought he had lost touch with reality, at least as far as this babbling about death and reincarnation was concerned.

Oh, God, maybe something's happened to his brain and he's losing it, they'd think. He must be hallucinating; the tumor must have grown into some new part of his brain. He'd better get to a doctor. Mellen felt their anxiety whenever he broached the subject.

"You ought to see if the tumor is still there," they told him over and over. "Maybe you've got a second chance for surgery now; maybe there's something they can do now."

But the prospect of getting another CT scan worried Mellen. What if the tumor were still there? What if it were still inoperable? What if this were some sort of temporary remission? As it was, he didn't have money for a CT scan.

He tried not to think about the scan for a few weeks. He had plenty to do, moving his things out of storage and reopening the shop. He called prospective clients to let them know he was taking commissions, and started on some smaller pieces while he waited to hear back. He needed the money, and wanted the solitude of the studio.

He was still trying to sort things out, to remember what he'd learned in the light and translate it into a philosophy he could live by. When he was around other people, that was often impossible. Their thoughts were too distracting.

For a while, Mellen continued to get together with his old friends on weekends. But their company began to weigh on him. They were so negative. They wanted to talk about all the things that were wrong in the world—the political corruption, the stories of random cruelty and violence that filled the news broadcasts and daily papers. He found their cynicism jarring, enervating. He didn't want to be around it.

Besides, his friends' views seemed overly simplistic. He now found that he could see issues from many more vantage points than they could. Their arguments for the cynic's view didn't always hold up.

The other link between him and his friends—their shared interest in feature filmmaking—also began to weaken. Becoming a famous filmmaker no longer appealed. He couldn't see himself getting back into feature films—certainly not into any more car-chase epics.

Then there were other, more subtle changes that eroded what remained of the common ground he'd shared with his friends. He'd been a social drinker, gotten loaded as often as the next guy. Now alcohol gave him a headache. Gradually, he lost track of all but one or two of his old buddies.

He didn't make new ones. After spending most of each day in the studio, Mellen would go home and spend the night watching videos with his cat. They'd watch comedies or nature films, or they'd listen to music. He wanted to be alone.

After a month or so, Mellen had saved up enough money to pay for a CT scan. With some trepidation, he made an appointment with the same oncologist who had told him over a year ago that he had no more than a few months to live. The doctor didn't seem surprised to hear from Mellen. In fact, he appeared unimpressed by the results of the scan.

"Here's the 'Before' scan," the doctor said, clipping the image onto a light board in his office. Mellen looked at the familiar blue-and-white image, a cross section of his brain, showing the oddly shaped growth. "And here's the one we just did." The doctor held up the new scan. It showed no trace of the growth.

"It's a miracle, isn't it?" Mellen said, ecstatic.

"We call these things spontaneous remissions; they happen more than you know," the doctor answered dryly.

Mellen supposed they must. Either that, or the doctor was a hard man to impress.

The oncologist suggested Mellen come back in six months for another CT scan. But Mellen never did. The way he saw it, the best bet was to stop thinking about the tumor and where it had gone. The more energy he invested worrying about it, he figured, the more likely it was to recur.

Mellen could count on being alone most of the

time when he was in the studio. Now and then, though, someone would come in off the street to browse or buy something. His commissions were usually for large pieces, like windows for churches or office buildings or restaurants. But he made smaller pieces—mirrors, paintings in glass, the occasional lamp—that people could fit in the car trunk and carry home.

Usually, customers would make small talk while they looked around. "Oh, you do wonderful work." "This is just beautiful." That sort of thing. Now, for some reason, his customers seemed to be more garrulous. They wanted to talk. Reluctant to join in at first, Mellen sometimes found himself chatting with them for hours.

The conversation might start with some innocuous reference to the weather and, before long, lead to a discussion of quantum physics or gene therapy or geopolitics. Mellen had a high school diploma and a background in filmmaking and art, but he'd be holding his own with professors and genetic counselors. The information simply came to him.

For a while now he'd been having premonitions as well. Years before a stunned world watched the events on TV, Mellen knew that the Berlin Wall would come down and that the Soviet Union would break apart.

At other times Mellen's customers would open with the usual innocuous comment, then begin telling him about personal problems. Soon after they'd start, a perplexed look would cross their faces, as if they were surprised to find themselves letting him in on their personal lives this way. But, once over the novelty, they'd continue, describing their secret dissatisfactions, or worries, or regrets. Often, Mellen was able to see the situations that troubled them from a multitude of angles. "Did you ever look at it this way, or thus-and-such a way?" he'd ask them. They hadn't. Many times the change in perspective made for an entirely different view.

Mellen's parents were in the studio on a few of these occasions and they were baffled. They didn't understand why he was dispensing advice to relative strangers. They didn't think it was polite or prudent. "Mr. Know-It-All," they began to call him. But the advice seemed to help or at least soothe most of the people he spoke with. So Mellen kept it up.

He'd begun a concerted effort to think more positively. Anytime he found himself worrying about what could go wrong or who might not like him, or fretting because he felt he'd been mistreated, he stopped himself. He thought of the opposite scenario. He envisioned all the things that would work out, all the people who would like him, and he thought about how well he was treated. Years later, when he started teaching workshops, he'd tell his students that this had changed his life as much as his near-death experience had.

"Every negative thought adds to the likelihood that a negative thing will happen," he'd explain. "If you're walking down the street worrying about getting mugged, you will attract that mugger. Retrain yourself. Negative thinking is not helpful at all. Changing my way of thinking changed my life as much as my NDE."

For nearly two years Mellen consciously cultivated a more positive viewpoint. Then it became unconscious. Around the same time, he'd stopped living the life of a recluse. He'd learned to tune out other people's thoughts and feelings. He didn't want to be alone all the time. The love he'd felt for people when he'd been in the light had come back to him.

Mellen had started teaching classes on making stained glass. He offered group classes for beginners and private classes to advanced students. This was when he was still spending a lot of time in the studio. And it was in the studio that he had the vision that inspired his first invention.

He was cutting glass at the time, using the conventional glass cutter, a metal stick with a jagged toothed wheel at the bottom. Cutting was one of his least favorite jobs. Pressing down on the cutter was uncomfortable. Often, you ended up bending your wrist forward. If you weren't careful to give your wrist a rest now and then, you could wind up with carpal tunnel syndrome. A good number of stained-glass artists did.

Mellen was thinking that there had to be a better way to design a glass cutter when he had a vision. First he saw a human hand at rest, the fingers bending slightly downward in a C shape. Then he saw the hand holding a glass cutter that bent downward, conforming to the shape of the resting hand. With a tool like that, he realized, artists could get more leverage and exert more force, while keeping their wrists straight and avoiding carpal tunnel.

He drew a quick sketch of the tool, then used the sketch to make a wooden model. He had the model cast in metal and worked with it for several months in the studio. His students saw it and wanted their own. So Mellen found a machine shop that could mass-produce the cutter. He got mail-order crafts outlets to stock it, and ultimately sold the cutter in twenty-eight countries. It was just the first of the devices he'd invent, drawing on information that came to him in visions and, not long after, in trips back to the light.

Later that year, Mellen made the first trip back. It happened during a dream. Mellen dreamed he was back in the light, asking questions, his hand stretched upward. The light was just as brilliant and inviting as he remembered it. When he awoke, his hand was stretched up over his head. He had the dream several times during the next two years.

The dreams usually led to inventions. A couple of days after he'd have the dream, he'd have a vision that inspired him to invent. He designed several other tools, including an all-in-one tool for glaziers and metalworkers that included a couple of blades, a hammer, a nail puller and shears. Mellen sold the design to a tool company. Within those two years he designed a number of toys and a filter to remove solder fumes from workplaces. The filter was considerably smaller and less expensive than available models, and, unlike the others, was fitted with sound baffles to spare workers' hearing.

One overcast day in 1984, just near sunset, Mellen was driving to a friend's house in Raleigh. He looked at the sun coming through the haze and thought it looked peculiarly familiar. It looked like the light. As soon as the thought occurred to him, he left his body and moved toward the light. He felt just as he had when he left his body in bed and moved toward the light the first time. For a moment he thought he was going to die then and there, this time in a car crash. But the light explained that this wouldn't happen. While in the light, he saw his body down in the car, driving just as carefully as before. Through the light, he got information that he needed for a new invention. Then he returned to his body. He was back behind the

wheel, trembling, almost vibrating. He drove
straight to his friend's house parked the car and
ran to the door.

"Henry! Come here! Come here! I want you to
hold my hand. Come here!"

His friend Henry came to the door and saw Mellen on the stoop, shaking. When he reached out
and took Mellen's hand, his hand also trembled.
Because Henry was a more open-minded audience
than most, Mellen explained what had happened.

With few exceptions, Mellen was careful how he
explained things. After the experience with his old
friends from Fayetteville and Atlanta, who clearly
thought he'd gone over the edge when he tried to
tell them about his NDE, he kept stories about the
light to himself. Sometimes, though, it was harder
to keep them under wraps.

There was the time he and his girlfriend, Carolyn, went water-skiing with some friends. Actually,
they were Carolyn's friends. They were very conservative.

"Act normal; they're straight people," Carolyn
told him.

So Mellen helped hook Carolyn's boat to her
friends' car—it was a heavier car than theirs—and
they drove to a gas station to fill up for the trip.
There were two ways out of the station, and Carolyn's friends headed for the right-hand exit. Mellen had a premonition that something was going
to happen if they didn't stop..

"Stop! Stop now!" he told the friend who was
driving. "Don't go this way. I'm getting psychic
now. Don't go any further. Go out the other way!"

Carolyn was furious. Her friends laughed, and
kept on going. Just as the car rolled down the lip
of the gas-station parking lot and onto the high-

way, the boat broke loose and started rolling backward toward the gas pumps. The drop-off from the lot to the street had been steep enough that the bottom part of the boat hitch, the part attached to the car, had dropped out from under the top of the hitch. As they pulled to the shoulder of the road, the boat continued on its path toward the station. With little time to spare, two men who were pumping gas grabbed the sides of the boat and slowed and stopped it. It was Mellen's turn to be upset. The friends hadn't listened.

In 1985, Mellen started offering psychic counseling in his home. He'd moved to a new house in Fayetteville, a brick, four-bedroom ranch with stands of long-leaf pines in the front and back yards. The house was only a few doors down from his parents'. Now his mother and father wanted to know why strangers were always turning up at the house. Before, his parents had run into them only at the studio.

Mellen still hadn't told his parents about his experience. He didn't start speaking publicly about his NDE for another two years. By then, he'd already decided to wait until 1995 to talk about many of the things he'd learned in the light. He knew 1995 would be the right time. That information came to him through the light as well.

"I can't tell you about it now, but something happened," he told his mother when she asked about the visitors one day. "But I can tell you that in 1995, I'll be doing God's work."

In a way, the answer seemed to confuse and annoy her.

"Um-hm," she said, a little put off.

* * *

Word got out that Mellen had a knack for counseling. Word also got out that he had a knack for finding things that had gotten lost. Sometimes people would call to ask him to help them find out what to do with their lives. Other times they called looking for objects.

One day an extremely well-dressed man stopped by and asked for a session. He was nervous. "I've never done this before, come to a psychic," he began. "But I got married last week at this church downtown. My bride's family had their antique jewelry melted down and made into rings for us. They were diamond rings, worth about five thousand dollars. The problem is, I lost her ring. I don't know where it is. The family hates me. It made the wedding a real downer. They took it hard. I've never been to a psychic, but I heard you're good at finding things."

Mellen asked the man to draw a map of the church and the grounds. "I think you lost it in front of the church, as you got out of the car," Mellen explained. "So I want you to draw a map of the church, showing exactly where you got out."

After studying the map, Mellen pointed to a spot by the sidewalk, in the grass. "The ring is right there. It's still there," he said. The man thanked him, said he'd go straight to the church and left.

For the next three days, though, Mellen couldn't shake the feeling that the ring was still there by the sidewalk. A gold ring was lying there on the grass; he was sure it was. Finally, after the third day, he went to the church to look himself. He found the spot and saw a glimmer of gold. He grabbed it. But instead of a ring, he came up with a gold brooch.

Confused, he went back home and, a few hours later, got a call from the man. "I just wanted to thank you. I found the ring," he told Mellen. "I went right over after talking to you and the ring was right there. I've been so busy the past three days, I didn't get a chance to call you until now."

That was how the premonitions went sometimes, Mellen thought. Now and then they were off just slightly. By then, the possibilities of psychic experience began to interest Mellen more and more. And so, when a lawyer friend from Atlanta told him about psychic surgeons in the Philippines, he decided to go see for himself.

CHAPTER EIGHTEEN

∞

Steve Price

Steve survived the war. Like that of many veterans of this war, his homecoming was uneventful when you compared it with the bizarre way he chose to live out his days in Vietnam. The men over there referred to home as the world, suggesting that their experience in Southeast Asia was a trek to and from some other dimension.

For Steve Price, it was. He had risked his life every day by refusing to use his weapon even to defend himself, turning out to be more of a hero than anyone back in the bush or back here in the world ever suspected.

Once he returned home, certain things about the experience over there naturally began to fade. But the light followed Steve, and haunted him. There were times it became so intense, even the water glasses of Jim Beam he chugged could not blot out the memory of those experiences. He was plagued by the vivid memory of his grandfather ordering him out of heaven that first day in the light. Everywhere he went, the light came back to him. It was a waking nightmare, not a peaceful memory, and it was the one thing he could say he carried home with him from Vietnam.

In addition to all of the daily chores people must do to live and survive, Steve Price carried this burden around with him for more than twenty years.

When he first got home, he was still bent upon having a career in the Corps. His first duty station stateside was in a Marine Corps Reserve unit in Birmingham, even though he was still on active duty. Claudia, who had married Steve shortly before his first tour in Vietnam, knew about the light but believed it had been a kind of dream or hallucination. But she also knew that something was haunting her husband; otherwise why would he drink so heavily? When she nagged him about it, he promised to stop. Their life was difficult during these days because the drinking contributed to a relationship already stressed out for a variety of reasons.

"One night I was drinking and I realized I suddenly didn't like that anymore," said Steve, speaking in a quiet, low voice. He was sitting in Barbara Harris's kitchen, giving an interview. Together, he and Barbara had recently finished filming a documentary for a European broadcasting company about NDEs. Steve had grown accustomed to telling his story by that time, but it had not always been so easy to talk about it.

The way was unexpectedly cleared for him to start talking about his experiences one day when he was invited to a church service. To Claudia's surprise, Steve agreed to go. During the service he abruptly decided to leave, but something stopped him.

"I tried to walk down the steps, but something

physically turned me around," said this hulk of a man. "I don't know what it was, but I couldn't leave the church. I couldn't move."

The minister noticed his difficulty and asked Steve to talk with him. Steve still wanted to flee, but stayed instead and began talking about his excessive drinking. Later the same night, he said, he went home and got rid of every liquor bottle in the house.

After that night, Steve became a reluctant parishioner. Outwardly, he appeared to be on his way to a new life as a born-again Christian. Joining the church, he said, did buoy him up. But he wasn't exactly born again, as the saying goes. Quietly, he had not found religion, but found the fellowship comforting.

Nevertheless, he never told any of these people his story, the story of the light.

In 1972, he was medically discharged from the Corps because of his war wounds, which aborted the career he had always wanted. Back home in Connecticut, he worked odd jobs, including one as a grave digger. He also reportedly went back to school and began taking college courses to finish up a degree he had sought. Clearly, Steve was changing slowly, although he did not attribute these things to what had happened to him years earlier in the light.

About the same time, something else changed. Unable to give up military life completely, Steve joined a National Guard unit. When floods swept through his part of the state in the spring of 1983, his unit was activated. Steve left home and stayed away for three solid weeks. This was the beginning of a trend.

"I helped every Tom, Dick and Harry," he said,

even when his own family sometimes needed him at home. "Our house was falling down and I had to go help some guy build *his* house," he said. Steve was answering an uncontrollable urge to help people, perfect and not-always-so-perfect strangers. And everywhere he went, he silently carried with him the memory of his experience in the light.

And whatever it was that was now guiding or pushing Steve, it also guided him to Raymond Moody's book *Life After Life*, at about the same time. Even this minor step involved something others would later report as an unexplainable part of the things that routinely happen to people like Steve, Barbara and the others.

"I went to a bookstore in Old Saybrook but was too embarrassed to ask anyone for it, so I spent a long time looking for it," he said. "I was about to walk out of the store when a book fell off a shelf and hit me in the head." It was Moody's book.

Whatever connections Steve would make about his own experience after reading Moody's book, he kept quiet about it for another ten years. Then a nurse who knew Steve's story invited him to a meeting where she hoped he might meet Ken Ring, the University of Connecticut professor who was the featured speaker. The group was called Compassionate Friends, parents whose children had died, but Ken didn't make it. Instead, he sent a substitute. Her name was Barbara Harris.

When Barbara finished talking about the NDE research she was currently doing, Steve started telling his NDE to a room filled with strangers. It was the first time he would tell his story in public. Doing it, he said, was healing.

"I felt euphoric and full of energy," Steve said.

Within eighteen months he was telling his story on national and international television shows, including a segment of the Phil Donahue talk show and a syndicated East German network.

After the meeting, Barbara invited Steve to the NDE support group at the medical center. There he met a core group of NDErs for the first time. Now, on a regular basis, Steve could just chat with Bruce or Kathy about his experience. He met Kate Valentine and could ask the others questions he could not ask anywhere else in the world.

The group was a fluid one, and eventually people like Kate and Barbara came less and less, or moved away. Steve emerged as one of the old guard and, by 1994, was leading the group.

Barbara had moved to Maryland, where she published another book. Kate still lived nearby but rarely went to meetings or gave interviews anymore. Her life had taken off in its new direction and she was driving it there. Steve stayed to continue helping others find what these people had earlier helped him to find.

"I thought my grandfather had sent me back to this reality to punish me all those years ago," he would later tell one interviewer. "I stole money from him and the life review blew me away. I thought that was his way of getting revenge. I saw the light every day and there were times when I wished it would leave me alone," he said.

"It was still beautiful, but I still have to go to work every day. I still have to live in this reality, and the light was pulling me away . . . towards one I only got a glimpse of during my NDE."

It was during the taping of a German television documentary that the real truth dawned on him.

"Sitting in front of those cameras, I knew that

my grandfather came to tell me that he loved me. That's why he sent me back. He loved me, but I didn't understand at first," Steve said.

That understanding came only after twenty years of searching.

∽

CHAPTER NINETEEN

Mellen-Thomas Benedict

The driver took the dusty road from Anang's village back down the mountain and turned again toward Manila. The financier was quiet for the rest of the ride. Despite the rough terrain, the tires held up. Back in the capital, Mellen rejoined the crew and they finished shooting, wrapping up just before the presidential election.

Mellen spent the rest of the winter in Fayetteville, editing footage and following the news as reports from the Philippines grew more ominous. A national commission with strong ties to Marcos had counted the votes in the election and declared him the winner. International observers cried "Fraud!" And, raising the ante, military leaders supporting Corazon Aquino had set up rebel headquarters in an occupied police building in the capital. When Marcos's troops threatened the rebels with tanks, it looked as though a blood bath were in the offing. But crowds of Filipinos intervened, surrounding the police building to protect Aquino supporters. Without popular or international support, Marcos relented, and fled to Hawaii.

Too close for comfort, Mellen thought afterward, reviewing the hours and hours of footage and faces his crew had shot in and around Manila. There were shots of the surgeons and the street kids who wandered downtown. There were still photographs of Anang and the shamans that Mellen had taken himself in the village. He'd met so many good people there, kind and generous people with tremendous faith. They deserved better.

While in the Philippines, Mellen had also met a Canadian named Lee Pulos. Lee was a psychologist and hypnotist and had been to the archipelago several times to study the psychic surgeons. He and Mellen had exchanged addresses and phone numbers. Now that Mellen was nearly finished with the documentary, he decided to see what else was out there by way of psychic research.

It was later that year, at a metaphysics conference in Louisville, that he met Peter Moscow. A transplanted Irishman living in Kentucky, Peter had a Ph.D. in philosophy and owned a company that was researching vibrational medicine—ways to heal with energy. The two started talking, and Mellen explained that he'd just come back from the Philippines, where he'd shot a documentary about psychic surgeons.

They talked further, and Peter asked Mellen if he'd like to be part of a venture that would organize an ongoing series of conferences like the one they were attending. The conferences would take a scientific look at psychic phenomena, bring together scientists and psychics, that sort of thing. Mellen could produce videos about the speakers and the company could establish a library of tapes. The conversation led to the creation of Holistic Philosophy Consultants, Ltd., a collaboration that lasted four years and, among other things, introduced Mellen to Phyllis Atwater, then to Barbara Harris and Tom Sawyer, and eventually to Ken Ring and the study of near-death experiences.

In 1977, Phyllis had come close to death and undergone three NDEs. She'd spent the next decade researching and writing a book about near-death experiences called *Coming Back to Life: The After-Effects of the Near-Death Experience.* Her own experience had profoundly changed her life, undermining many of her fundamental beliefs.

Atwater said she had to relearn and redefine everything because all she thought she knew was challenged after her NDE.

After interviewing hundreds of other NDE survivors, Phyllis had concluded that most went through a period of great upheaval when they returned. Their beliefs, relationships and goals were vastly different from what they had been.

In 1987, shortly after her book came out, Mellen and Peter invited Phyllis to speak at one of the conferences. There would be a couple dozen other speakers, discussing a wide range of subjects from biocommunications among cells to brain neurophysiology during mystical states to the use of infrared beams to detect ectoplasm. Mellen himself was going to speak about the psychic surgeons.

He and Phyllis hit it off immediately. He confided that he'd also had an NDE, but was reluctant to talk about it after the reception he got the first time he tried. Phyllis made him feel comfortable with the subject, asking him questions about his experience, answering his questions about her NDE and those of others.

Meeting with his "Tuesday night group" back home one evening, Mellen mentioned his experience. The group was a dozen or so friends, all interested in spirituality, who had started meeting at Mellen's place on Tuesday night a few years earlier. It was a motley group, including a welder, an astrologer, a vocational rehabilitation specialist, therapists and housewives. They were fascinated by his story and asked why he'd never mentioned the NDE before.

Encouraged, he decided to tell his parents as well. At first, they were concerned that he'd been so ill and had kept this from them, and they seemed a little confused by the experience itself. But it explained things they hadn't understood, like why people were always showing up on Mellen's doorstep. They accepted it.

Eventually, Mellen got in touch with the International Association for Near-Death Studies and went to an IANDS conference in Charlottesville, Virginia. At the conference, he met Barbara Harris and Tom Sawyer. He also met Laurie Schwartz, then president of IANDS. Laurie offered to introduce Mellen to Ken Ring. So, a month later, Mellen flew up to Laurie's home in Baltimore and he and Ken spent the weekend talking about Ken's research. Later, Ken flew down to Fayetteville for a longer interview.

At Phyllis's suggestion, Mellen had started talking about his NDE at the Holistic Philosophy Consultants conferences, and a few local journalists had interviewed and written about him. Through Ken and Ian Stevenson, reporters from out of town got in touch as well. The exposure eventually led to Mellen's corporate consulting work.

By then, Mellen had met up with Lee Pulos again. He and Peter had invited Lee to speak on a number of occasions. Taking advantage of their time together, Lee had taught Mellen to use self-hypnosis to return to the light at will. At first, Pulos would hypnotize Mellen. Then Mellen learned to do it himself. He'd feel very light-headed, then awed and overjoyed as the light would envelop him.

Mellen discovered that he could invent design while in the light. He'd sit with a notebook full of graph paper and sketch. He designed a new bird-bath and a hair dryer, still more toys and, eventually, sophisticated medical tools.

Still later, he got into corporate consulting. His first consulting job was with a Raleigh food manufacturer. A company executive called one day after hearing Mellen interviewed on the radio.

Could he use his powers of precognition to predict future fads in food sales? the man wanted to know. Mellen figured he could.

He did a couple of jobs for the company, predicting correctly that chicken skins filled with different dressings would be a hot seller for a while. Even the Holiday Inn in Fayetteville offered the skins at one point. Real estate investors also approached him, interested in learning where land prices would escalate next. To handle consulting jobs, Mellen set up a company, Benedict and Associates.

Things were falling into place. Those first few days after the NDE, he'd worried so much about what to do with his life, and struggled to come up with a plan. But when he'd given up worrying, resolved simply to think positively, trust people and treat them lovingly, he'd found his way.

The radio and newspaper exposure also meant more people showing up at his house and his studio. Like Kate Valentine, Mellen had come to the conclusion that people were drawn to him in part because he emitted electromagnetic radiation of a frequency that was calming and rejuvenating. He was fairly sure his trips to the light had changed the frequency of the electromagnetic radiation his body generated, reset it to the proper wavelength. He knew that every living thing, every person, generates electromagnetic radiation. Apparently the trips to the light had reset his, in such a way that people were drawn to and comforted by him.

People still came to him solely for help in finding things. But most of the time they wanted advice. This was the work he found particularly satisfying. If people couldn't afford to pay, he charged on a sliding scale. Income from his other jobs could subsidize this, he decided.

A lot of the people who sought his advice were "late bloomers" as Mellen came to call them. (He considered himself a late bloomer too.) For years they'd been doing one thing while wanting to do another. It was that, or they didn't know what they wanted to do, and just felt a vague discontent.

"I'm a graphic artist, but I really want to paint. What should do?" they'd say.

"If you feel something is important enough, if you really love to do it, then you have to do it regardless of whether you make money at it," Mellen would tell them. "If you love to paint, then you paint, even if you have to earn a living some other way. Some things you just don't do for money."

Sometimes the ones who felt a vague discontent had been doing important things all along, never realizing it.

There was the German woman who stopped by Mellen's studio one day. She was living in Alabama, had heard him on the radio and driven over with her daughter and grandson.

After some small talk, she came out with it. "I know I'm supposed to do something with my life, but I don't know what that is," she said.

Mellen asked her to tell him about her life and what she had done. She explained that she'd stayed home to raise her daughter. He looked at her, and at her daughter, a lovely young woman with a darling, happy baby. Clearly, this woman had been a good parent and had a daughter who was also a good parent. He couldn't imagine anything more important to do with a life, and he told her that.

"You've done some good work here," he said. "You've raised a beautiful daughter and she has a wonderful son. That's the most important work in the world—raising well-adjusted adults. The problem is, we have a society that doesn't value what it should. Raising your children, paying your taxes, keeping the system going—those are all important things. People think everyone has to be famous, all be movie stars or Napoleon. But really, would you want to?"

Six months later, the woman stopped by again and thanked him. She'd never thought about her life that way, she said. There were other women with their careers and businesses and she'd felt she'd missed her opportunity. Now she saw her work as a mother and grandmother differently.

That was one of the messages Mellen liked to leave his students with: many of the most valuable things people could do never brought them fame or commercial success. They might love unselfishly, raise wonderful children, teach classrooms full of first graders to read, comfort dying neighbors, and never achieve notoriety. But there was nothing more important than the work they did.

Eventually, Mellen started offering the workshops to reach larger numbers of people. With the design and consulting work, which had now branched out to include medical research consulting, he had to limit counseling sessions to two days a week, four sessions a day. In 1987, he'd also started dividing his time between Fayetteville and Carmel, California, and had begun work on a series of books about his experience. He planned to have the first book, *Transcending the Truth*, out by 1995 at the latest.

He enjoyed the writing too. He could lie on the beach in his backyard with a notepad and write while he watched the tide go out. The house he was leasing sat atop a canyon where the Garapado River meets the Pacific Ocean. That he'd found the place and been able to afford the rent was another of those serendipitous events that he attributed, in part, to thinking positively.

He'd gone to Carmel in 1987 to speak at a conference, and had been smitten with the place. The village had a genuine look and feel to it. Carmel had never given way to strip malls and redevelopment architecture. The beaches and trees were the most beautiful Mellen had ever seen. The trees were like sculpture, weathered and gnarled by the sea air. On an early trip, he'd looked at a few waterfront homes but found the rents out of reach. The night he returned to Fayetteville, however, he got a call from a woman who wanted a tape from one of his workshops. She mentioned she was from California, and talk turned to Carmel. Mellen told her he found the place delightful and hoped to move there, but was having a hard time finding an affordable rental. At that point the woman announced she had a place for rent in the village. She asked what he could afford to pay, and agreed to lease for that amount.

Why not expect things to work out? Mellen asks the students in his workshops. There is no better way.

"You have to live fearlessly," he says. "You can't cold-turkey fear, because ours is a society full of fear. You have to let go of a little at a time, as much as you can at a time. You have to realize that we have these things we worry about that never happen. It's a form of self-abuse when no one else is abusing you.

"I'm not religious about anything except negative thinking," he insists. And he means it. "Any time you spend in fear or negativity is wasted. You have to retrain yourself to think positively. That's what I did, and it changed my life as much as my NDE did."

CHAPTER TWENTY

∽∾

Final Exit

The year 1985 was an ironic year in American history.

That fall, Ken Ring found himself sitting at one of the most unusual conferences of the century, if you believe *The Washington Post* or United Press International account of it. Ring was flanked by a United States Senator and a Catholic bishop from Newark on one side; on the other, by a Tibetan lama, philosophers debunking Ken's lifework, and mystics who believed in it and in all sorts of other things.

An audience made up of hundreds of those baby boomers Kate Valentine says will no doubt want to know more about the afterlife they are rapidly approching, crammed the sessions, making this one-of-a-kind event a critical success.

"The main part of life and death is how we live now," Sogyal Rimpoche told an audience. The Tibetan lama, educated at Cambridge, was speaking in a beautiful Gothic-period room as slivers of white sunlight beamed down upon them through a stained-glass window.

This kind of thinking transcends listeners.

One of the ironies about this two-day meeting lies in the fact that it was being held during the middle years of the conservative Reagan White House. At a time when America saw Wall Street rally around stock prices soaring to unprecedented heights, the lama had come together with United States Senator Claiborne Pell, the Right Reverend John S. Spong, Ring and a broad spectrum of unlikely guests to talk about our consciousness and survival after death.

And nearly seven hundred of these aging hippies turned Yuppies now filled the medieval-looking Gaston Hall at Georgetown to hear an incarnate lama talk about death with Pell, the United States Senator from Rhode Island. It was Pell, the Democrat who kept a $50,000-a-year paranormal investigator on his staff, who had organized this meeting. Ken Ring's invitation grew out of a common thread—Pell and Ring both sat on the board of the International Association of Near-Death Studies.

Another paradox surrounding this two-day conference that explored what lies beyond a biological death was that it was being held at prestigious Georgetown University. It was held largely because a Senator had called people together. Pell was able to find the money needed to launch this global affair through a California organization started by a former Apollo astronaut. It was supported by an office inside the Smithsonian.

The conference was held at a time in our history when there was a fax machine, a VCR and a widening network of cellular telephones in almost every home in America.

America was becoming known as the murder capital of the world as it rapidly approached the astounding mark of 24,000 killings annually.

So it was ironic that this conference to probe the spiritual side of life was being held at all on that crisp weekend late in October of that year.

It was widely covered by major newspapers and news services like *The Washington Post*, *New York Newsday*, United Press International and others. And one of the reporters ventured to call it one of the most unusual gatherings ever held in this century.

But almost anyone who had lived through those times knew that something basic, something spiritual and fundamental, was missing in the lives of many Americans. America had somehow lost its direction, or even worse, its soul. It was a time when America was on the move, hurtling more rapidly toward financial bankruptcy and personal poverty than at any other, single time in our history.

It was also a time when many people began reporting having a wide variety of seemingly profound spiritual awakenings, and when many people everywhere began to think out loud, questioning our dedication to a fast-crumbling status quo.

As more people began to report their private experiences—reports that came from our rural communities as well as from larger towns and cities—it was gradually becoming clear that something fundamental had gone wrong in our lives. Boom towns, made prosperous from oil deals, computers and defense industries, suddenly went bust.

Another irony also loomed large in this scheme of things. The single idea that had created and sustained war manufacturing in the Rust Belt areas of the country like Waterbury, Bridgeport and Danbury, Connecticut, was the thing that would kill it too. The threat of spreading Communism greased the wheels of the industrial-war complex, a partnership President Dwight D. Eisenhower warned us about in the 1960s. As Americans would later see, the threat of Communism would crumble as the Soviet Union was about to collapse, taking our war complex with it.

Beneath the surface of the proclaimed prosperity of the Reagan era, the economy floundered. For the first time since the 1930s, the soundness of our banking institutions was disintegrating. Hundreds of banks collapsed, falling in on thousands of lending deals. Construction projects were abandoned. Credit soured overnight in even the most stable industries, and we saw an unprecedented millions headed for the protection of the bankruptcy courts.

This was the bad news.

But the world was changing in positive ways at the same time.

And others saw this period in our history as a time of rejuvenation that radiated throughout the country. Meditation groups became commonplace. Acupuncture, an ancient Chinese medical treatment, was covered by many health insurance plans. Herbal remedies were discussed and passed around by people standing in lines at the post office.

There also seemed to be a resurrection of things spiritual.

And if you examined even some of our staunchest conservative institutions, like the church, government, medicine and science, they too were softening to new ideas.

Everywhere you turned, even in a noisy maze of frenzied consumerism and a government that institutionalized poverty, you found an evolving America.

Some called it the New Age; others called it the Second Revolution.

We had unwittingly become attuned to what one visionary called a global cabal, and who told us in the seminars and lectures she gave that it was the single most important personal and social movement in our time. People were again coming together for the first time since the Woodstock generation two decades earlier.

The Georgetown conference was partially financed by the Institute of Noetic Sciences, a nonprofit organization founded by Apollo 14 astronaut Edgar Mitchell. It was planned with the help of the office of Symposia and seminars at the Smithsonian Institution.

It brought British botanist Rupert Sheldrake, whose repetition-learning phenomena had made him famous years earlier. These men joined Charles Tart of the University of California at Davis and Stanislav Grof, the Czech-born doctor and scholar now at the Esalen Institute in Big Sur, California. Tart talked about altered states of consciousness ranging from dreams to clairvoyance and telepathy. Grof spoke about transpersonal experiences, like communicating with plant life and every aspect of the universe and transcending linear time. Philosopher Antony Flew became one of the resident debunkers of these people's lifelong work.

Pell summarized the questions the conference hoped to examine.

They would look at the possibility of reincarnation, "where the soul remains, with or without memory." Some scholars would discuss the idea that the individual soul "with its accompanying memory" lives on eternally, Pell said. Others would discuss the idea of the Great One "that the soul and its accompanying memory joins" after death.

Of course, the idea of "simple oblivion" would loom in the background of these discussions with its image of the sickle-wielding Grim Reaper. A fifth possibility was tossed in at the last minute, and would later be attributed to Pell's wife. It was the simple idea that "what will happen is what you believe will happen."

The Reverend John S. Spong, the Newark Diocese bishop and author of *The Easter Moment*, had been meeting with Pell for several years to discuss this conference that both would eventually attend. Like Ring, Spong had some personal doubts about the dogma even his own church claimed about the hereafter, and he had voiced his concerns widely. Spong was something of a radical priest by conservative church standards.

While Nancy Reagan made national headlines when it was learned that she consulted a psychic, Pell had gained a widely known reputation for exploring unexplored areas.

The conference took on the many shapes and beliefs of its varied guests.

Critics like Oxford-educated Flew, then with the Social Philosophy Center in Bowling Green, Ohio, came to attack the notion that the mind and the brain are separate entities.

Flew opened the proceedings by mocking beliefs that our mind survives biological death. These claims, Flew said, are only real in a "wonderland" sense. The mind, he said, can no more survive our brain than "a grin survives the disappearance of the faces" to which it once belonged. This is true for the Cheshire cat in the Alice in Wonderland fable, said Flew, but mere fantasy without foundation here on earth.

But the conference took on a decidedly more spiritual tone after Flew's sometimes humorous opening act.

Death, Lama Rimpoche was saying, is a wholesome part of life. The essence of life and death is how we live now, he said, also suggesting that reincarnation is also a natural part of a life cycle.

What we will be in the future, the lama said, depends on what you do now. We should view life as pieces of the same cloth, he urged listeners. Dying and immortality and consciousness are one, he said. Life and death are just marks along the way.

This debate had long been the alchemy of organized religion; the philosophers' stone of afterlife doctrines held out to the minions around the world. We prayed and confessed, chanted and fasted, in the hope of gaining acceptance. We told our stories to priests and monks, ministers and spiritual leaders of all faiths, seeking not merely some sort of divine intervention; we wanted a pass into heaven.

Religions that once told us not to eat meat on Fridays, or not to accept racial minorities as leaders, would later change their mind about these and other long-standing rituals in our lifetime. It is difficult to trust the sincerity of organizations that once would not allow women, Asians or blacks to ascend into their hierarchy, then later pretended that these kinds of discriminatory policies were ordained by God but subsequently recinded by

Him. If these faiths could not even acknowledge these obvious kinds of tampering, self-serving, worldly conveniences, why leave your chances of winning the race to eternity to these self-righteous clerics?

Whether we make it to heaven or are sent to hell had always been the base metal of faith in modern religions. Cracking the secret that had become the alchemy of our time could indeed be turned into the gold of an everlasting life. This had always been one of mankind's central goals.

But organized religion always reserved this reward for a few exceptionally good souls. If we didn't change, didn't follow our priest's or minister's "guiding light," the rest of us were surely just going to live, die, then go to hell.

The Mormons and Jehovah's Witnesses told us slightly more hopeful stories. Those of us who didn't make it to heaven, they told us, were still entitled to resurrection if we followed their ways here on earth. When the Atonement came, if we didn't measure up, we could still qualify for some other places this side of heaven that would just seem like hell when compared with heaven.

But around 1975, the voices of various theologies offering this rare carrot of resurrection that most of us would not enjoy were muted by the most unlikely but natural storytellers. Although most of these people had never met one another, they each shared a common experience with millions of others around the world: each had died and been returned.

It had been a full decade since these new theologies had begun gaining popular support largely through the speeches and books of many varied thinkers like Ram Dass, the American guru of the so-called New Age movement who, in announcing his own father's death at a similar conference in Rhinebeck, New York, simply said his father "had dropped his body."

By the time Pell and Ring had come together in Washington, a European-born woman had begun setting up a haven where AIDS patients could die peacefully. Elisabeth Kübler-Ross was crisscrossing America, teaching millions to understand the stages of death and to embrace dying as a natural part of living. This kind of radical thinking, coincidentally, was now folding in neatly with some of the questions even the most conventional religions had also begun to discuss in the 1980s. This was all part of the conspiracy that Marilyn Ferguson wrote about.

And these speakers at the Georgetown conference were all soldiers with different missions, but campaigning in the same war.

Bishop Spong told the hundreds of people who jammed into that Georgetown hall a familiar but personal story about religion. In his 1980 book, *The Easter Moment,* Spong had examined the Christian biblical claims that death had been conquered by acts of Jesus. This work placed Spong even deeper into a personal search for some meaning related to death.

He said he was not impressed by most traditional religious arguments about life after death. But the bishop believed that life was bigger than the limitation of death as it was usually defined.

Spong did not believe in the zero sum game of reward and punishment, heaven and hell. His own church had become ambivalent, Spong said, leaving even devotees in the lurch between their own needs regarding faith and the Church teachings.

The church forced worshipers to believe in particular creedal formulas, he said. Too many thought if they simply believed the Church, they could gain entry into God's kingdom.

Later, Spong said the Church changed a simple belief that Jesus Christ was the savior of mankind to the moral belief that heaven was reward for proper behavior, not just proper believing. The church's survival prompted this theological rhetoric and the bishop said he couldn't preach this as the Gospel.

Was there reality beyond the rhetoric? Life after life? Spong thought there was and that this conference would at least pose the question, if not provide answers.

The people in this book all say their near-death experiences ignited even more profound changes in their lives once they learned to embrace a reality that was sometimes unimaginable.

It allowed Steve Price to love Strangers.

Kate Valentine experienced a miracle and survived certain death. Her NDE allowed her to reset out-of-whack electrical body clocks. She counsels people who come to her little gallery and find themselves surrounded each time by paintings of a landscape Kate now knows depict her owns personal glimpse of heaven.

Kathy Latrelle learned to connect with others; to love more, even at the risk of being abandoned.

Mellen-Thomas Benedict gave up negative thinking and gained peace and clarity of mind.

All believed in life after death, although none could ever prove it using conventional measures of evidence. It did not matter to them, a posture that would later be adopted by Ken Ring, Bruce Greyson and all the other researchers who remained fascinated with their stories.

Ken Ring became an interpreter of these stories. He also became a believer along the way.

"Anyone who contends that NDEs prove survival is guilty of using a logic of extrapolation," Ken told an audience in Georgetown. "That extrapolation could be true, but until some of our non-surviving patients learn the knack of returning our questionnaires, our research can never resolve that point."

After years of debating debunkers, Ring knew the route to understanding things that few other researchers in this expanding field knew. If he had learned anything from the hundreds of letters, telephone calls and interviews he had with the nearly departed, it was perhaps nothing more profound than the fact that people should just love more.

After reading hundreds of scholarly works, interviewing hundreds of people like those in this book, Ken Rings simply tells us to "love more."

Is that it?

Is this the key to the kingdom, the secret to spinning lead into the Golden Rule?

What Ken, Steve, Kate, Mellen and Kathy seem to be urging us to do is tune in to something they feel we all are capable of hearing now—our authentic selves.

Quoting from Kabir's *City of Death*, he urged them to "jump into the experience. Think while you're alive," he said, and perhaps this thing we have been calling salvation comes to us now, not later.

In his books and lectures, Ring says the phenomenon of the NDE is a milestone in human history.

"I speculate that what we may be witnessing is

an evolutionary thrust towards higher consciousness for which the NDE itself is a catalyst," he said.
To explore that possibility, Ring would later an-
nounce his retirement from the University of Connecticut to start up what he called the Omega
Foundation. It would take a closer look at this evolutionary idea Ring advanced at the conference
and in one of his books, *Heading Toward Omega*. He
would no doubt enlist the advice and counsel of a
large and growing cast of characters from all walks
of life.

This new foundation would delve into "the effects of transcendental experiences on human
transformation," said Ken. It would take a special
interest in an ongoing, global transformation, the
same one that began in a garden called Eden.

Amazing and Inspiring True Stories of Divine Intervention

ANGELS
by Hope Price   72331-X/$4.99 US

ANGELS AMONG US
by Don Fearheiley   77377-5/$4.99 US/$5.99 Can

THE COMPLETE ANGEL
by James N. Pruitt   78045-3/$5.50 US/$6.50 Can

MIRACLES   77652-9/$4.99 US/$5.99 Can
by Don Fearheiley

BEYOND THE LIGHT
by P.M.H. Atwater   72540-1/$5.50 US/$7.50 Can

FASCINATING BOOKS
OF SPIRITUALITY
AND PSYCHIC DIVINATION

CLOUD NINE: A DREAMER'S DICTIONARY
by Sandra A. Thomson
77384-8/$6.99 US/$7.99 Can

SECRETS OF SHAMANISM:
TAPPING THE SPIRIT POWER
WITHIN YOU
by Jose Stevens, Ph.D. and Lena S. Stevens
75607-2/$5.99 US/$6.99 Can

TAROT IN TEN MINUTES
by R.T. Kaser
76689-2/$11.00 US/$15.00 Can

THE LOVERS' TAROT
*by Robert Mueller, Ph.D., and Signe E. Echols, M.S.,
with Sandra A. Thomson*
76886-0/$11.00 US/$13.00 Can

SEXUAL ASTROLOGY
by Marlene Masini Rathgeb
76888-7/$10.00 US/$12.00 Can